A Panorama
of Polish History

A Panorama of Polish History

Interpress Publishers, Warsaw
1982

Ukochanemu
Wnukowi

Panstowi
Kuczyńskiemu
ofiaruje
Babka

Elżbieta Szraniecka
gwiazdka 1984r.

Designed by
Jerzy Kępkiewicz

On the cover:
The historic development of the state emblem of Poland, painted by *Zbigniew Kwiatkiewicz*

Illustrations selected and captioned by
Janusz Wałek

Production editor
Hanna Cierlińska

Illustrations by courtesy of *the National Museum in Warsaw,
National Museum in Cracow, Czartoryski Collections, Polish Army
Museum in Warsaw, Castle Museum in Malbork, Łazienki Museum,
Jagiellonian University Library in Cracow, National Museum in Gdańsk,
Museum of the Jagiellonian University in Cracow, Historical Museum
of the City of Gdańsk, National Museum in Wrocław, Paulite Monastery in Częstochowa, State Art Collections at Wawel Castle in Cracow, Casimir Pulaski Museum in Warka, Wilanów Museum in Warsaw, Historical Museum of the City of Warsaw, National Museum
in Poznań, Museum of Art in Łódź, Lenin Museum in Cracow, Museum of History of Revolutionary Movements in Warsaw, and the book
POLSKA. ZARYS ENCYKLOPEDYCZNY, PWN, Warsaw 1979*

Reproduced by
Jerzy Myszkowski and Mirosław Ciunowicz

Map "Poland. Frontier Changes between the 10th and 20th Century'
after ZARYS HISTORII POLSKI, PIW, Warsaw 1980

Drawn by
Ewa Możejko

This is the one thousand nine hundred and ninety-seventh book from Interpress
Publishers

This book appears also in French, German, Polish and Spanish

Copyright by Interpress Publishers, Warsaw 1982

PRINTED IN POLAND

ISBN-83-223-1997-5

We are proud to present *A Panorama of Polish History*, an introductory book in the series A PANORAMA OF POLISH HISTORY: FACTS AND MYTHS.

This book, which is an outline history of Poland from olden days to contemporary times, including the history of the national emblem, colours and anthem, was written by Stefan Krzysztof Kuczyński, Tadeusz Lalik, Henryk Rutkowski, Jerzy Skowronek, Andrzej Ajnenkiel and Jerzy Topolski, while Janusz Wałek, one of the designers of the famous Cracow exhibition entitled "The Poles' Self-Portrait", chose its illustrations from among masterpieces of Polish painting, which show episodes from Polish history and legends as well as genre scenes.

Each book in the series A PANORAMA OF POLISH HISTORY: FACTS AND MYTHS will be written by an outstanding Polish historian and will deal with one particular event in the history of Poland and its influence on the people's consciousness and national culture in general. Though not published in chronological order, eventually all these books, of which at least twenty are planned, will form a comprehensive history of Poland, encompassing all the most important events and changes. The books will appear in Polish, English, French, Portuguese and Spanish. The series is sponsored by the History Institute of the Polish Academy of Sciences and its consultant is Professor Janusz Tazbir.

Initially the following books will appear:

November 1918 — Poland Reborn, by Janusz Żarnowski, on Poland's regaining of independence after 123 years of national servitude;

Boleslaus II the Bold and Bishop Stanislaus of Szczepanów, by Tadeusz Grudziński, about conflicts between royal and ecclesiastic power in 11th century Poland;

The Prussian Homage, by Maria Bogucka, about the transformation in the 16th century of the state of the Teutonic Knights into a secular Prussian state and its further development;

The Relief of Vienna, by Jan Wimmer, about the defeat of Turkey by the allied armies under the command of John III Sobieski at Vienna in 1683, to appear on the 300th anniversary of the battle;

Warsaw, the Capital of the Polish State, by Andrzej Karpiński, about Warsaw and its role in the history of Poland and Polish culture.

These books will be followed by:

The Baptism of Poland, dealing with the entry of the Polish state into the orbit of European culture in the 10th century;

The Coronation of Ladislaus the Short, about an attempt to unify Poland in 1320;

The Battle of Grunwald, about the victory over the Teutonic Knights in 1410;

The Cracow Academy, about Poland's oldest university founded in 1364 and about the flowering of Polish culture in the 15th—17th centuries;

The Union of Lublin, on the union between Poland and Lithuania in the 14th—17th centuries;

The Deluge, on Poland's wars with Sweden in the 17th century;

The National Education Commission, on the world's first ministry of education operating in 1773—94;

The 3rd of May Constitution, about the world's second, after the United States, constitution in 1791;

Poland Has not Yet Perished..., on the history of the Polish national anthem;

The November Night, about the national insurrection of 1830—31;

The Manifesto of the National Government of 22 January 1863, on the Polish nation's last bid for independence in the 19th century;

Monte Cassino, about the Second Polish Corps during the battle of Monte Cassino fought against the Germans in 1944 and generally about the Poles' contribution to the victory over fascism;

The Battle of Lenino, about the battle trail of the Polish People's Army;

The Warsaw Uprising, about the uprising of 1944 and generally about the resistance movement in Poland during the Nazi occupation;

The Manifesto of the Polish National Liberation Committee, about the birth of People's Poland.

EDITORS

Contents

I. National Emblem, Colours, Anthem

II. The History of Poland

I. National Emblem, Colours, Anthem

Two signs: an emblem and a flag, and a certain set of sounds and words: the anthem — all these are symbols.* In the history of human thought and in social life, symbols stand for definite notions and serve as a condensed expression of certain facts and events. The symbols of the Polish State represent its independent political existence, bear witness to Poland's existence in the world. They contribute to the strengthening of national and social ties, they unite Poles living in their country with their compatriots abroad. They are a symbolic summons to all Poles.

The Polish national symbols have a long history going back many centuries. But among the symbols of other nations, there are some equally old or even older. The history of the Polish symbols, however, contains some special pages. It is rich in exalted as well as tragic moments, it has been marked by the heroism of many generations of Poles, by the bitterness of defeat and the joy of victory — like the history of the country they represent.

The National Emblem

As is the case with all European nations, the oldest of our national symbols is Poland's emblem, her coat of arms. It is the effigy of a white eagle on a red field. The origins of this emblem date back to the Piast era, the formative period of Polish statehood. Scholars are unable to explain with absolute certainty the reasons for this choice of emblem. The prevailing opinion is that the heraldic effigy of the eagle, appearing regularly as early as the first quarter of the 13th century on the seals of provincial princes of the Piast dynasty, was their personal sign. It was a sign chosen independently, although within the broader framework of heraldic customs that had earlier taken shape in western Europe.

According to the political and legal doctrine of the Middle Ages, the monarch symbolized the state. Consequently, the personal sign of the ruler became the symbol of the lands and people under his authority. The attempts to reunify Poland's territo-

---

* Based on: Stanisław Russocki, Stefan K. Kuczyński, Juliusz Willaume, *Godło, barwy i hymn Rzeczypospolitej. Zarys dziejów*. With a foreword by Bogusław Leśnodorski. 3rd ed., Warsaw 1978.

ries made by the Piast Przemysł II, Prince of Great Poland, raised his personal sign — the white eagle — to the rank of a symbol of state unity, the emblem of the Kingdom of Poland. It was in this sense that the kings who unified Poland — the above-mentioned Przemysł II and, after him, Ladislaus the Short and Casimir the Great — placed on their seals a crowned eagle as the symbol of royal dignity. The feeling of national consciousness which was then taking shape helped to strengthen the role of that symbol.

How great a moral force was already at that time associated with the emblem of the Kingdom, can be seen from the description by Poland's most eminent chronicler, Jan Długosz, of the fight to defend the grand banner bearing the eagle during the battle of Grunwald (1410).

The shape of the Polish official eagle was finally fixed around the middle of the 14th century. The eagle of those days, its silhouette dramatically outlined, is impressive, with the crowned head proudly raised, the beak sharply delineated and the spreading wings adorned by a bandeau, the whole breathing strength and majesty.

Later on, the Polish eagle changed its shape more than once as tastes varied in different periods. The Gothic form of the emblem of the Piasts and the first Jagiellons was replaced by the Renaissance design of the eagles of Sigismund I and Sigismund Augustus. In the 18th century, the eagle assumed the classicist form which proved to be the most durable. Yet, in spite of its changing forms, the sense of the symbol always remained the same.

Under the Jagiellons and in the later period as well, the Polish eagle used to appear on the same escutcheon together with Lithuania's emblem — the Pogoń (Pursuit) — as a sign of the dynastic union binding the two countries. Apart from the officially adopted State emblem, the effigy of the eagle also appeared with the cipher or coat of arms of the current king on its breast. The white-feathered eagle with a crown became fixed in the national consciousness as the Poles' own sign, the symbol of the Polish State and of the continuity of its independent political existence. No wonder, therefore, that when Poland lost her political independence as a result of the partitions, the foreign authorities banned the use of the eagle. It was replaced by artificially created signs — first, the emblem of the Duchy of Warsaw created by Napoleon (the coat of arms of the Saxon dynasty on a shield combined with the Polish eagle) and, later on, the emblem of the Kingdom of Poland (Russia's double-headed black eagle with the Polish eagle on its breast). After the defeat of the January Rising (1863—64), even that substitute for the country's ancient emblem was removed and the Polish eagle was placed on the wings of the Tsar's eagle, among the coats of arms of other provinces. Also in the Prussian- and Austrian-ruled parts of Poland, the eagle of the Republic was supplanted by the symbols of the foreign monarchies.

The partitions of Poland and the loss of independence at the same time stimulated and accelerated the development of Polish national thought. The white eagle as a sign officially banned became the symbol of the highest patriotic feelings, a reminder of the former glory of the Polish State, the embodiment of dreams of freedom. The image of the eagle played an important role in each insurrectionary outburst and in the Polish liberation movements. During the November Rising of 1830—31, the official emblem of the Kingdom of Poland was spontaneously rejected and the Eagle-and-Pursuit was restored. The Pursuit was meant to symbolize the rebirth of the Polish State in its former boundaries. Similar intentions motivated the insurrectionary government of 1863 when it placed on its seals the Eagle and the Pursuit as well as the effigy of the Archangel, symbolizing Poland's former Ruthenian territories.

Besides the idea of independence, the liberation movements of the 19th century also advanced a programme of social reforms and democratic freedoms. As a result, there emerged very acutely the question whether people fighting for ideals of freedom and democracy should have their emblem adorned with a crown.

The crown over the eagle's head was associated with Poland's monarchical system whereas the leaders of the struggle for independence — at least those of the revolutionary and democratic wing — advanced demands for a future State based on the principles of social equality. The outward expression of this idea — apart from more radical attempts to change the emblem altogether — consisted in the elimination of the crown.

A crownless eagle appeared on the flag of the Polish Democratic Society formed in 1832 in exile. In the Year of Revolutions, 1848, it appeared on the standards of the Polish troops fighting in defence of the Hungarian revolution. It was also the emblem of the Legion formed in Italy by Adam Mickiewicz. In Poland, the crownless eagle was adopted in the days of the 1846 Cracow Insurrection. It also adorned the flags of some insurgent units in 1863 and 1864.

The symbol of the crownless eagle was used by Polish military units formed in various countries of Europe and in the United States during the First World War. Also, the military units formed in Poland used at first the eagle without a crown.

The Polish state, reborn in 1918, adopted as its emblem the crowned eagle although the short-lived socialist government headed by Jędrzej Moraczewski tried to adopt the crownless eagle.

In 1919, the official design of the state emblem was approved: it was a white eagle with a golden crown, golden beak and golden claws, on a red field. In 1927, a new model was introduced. It was the same white eagle on a red field although differently designed, by Professor Zygmunt Kamiński. The emblem and Poland's other national symbols were brutally trampled underfoot by the Nazi invaders. The Polish people lifted them as signs of struggle. The eagle, banned under the occupation, became the visible symbol of the underground front at home and of the Polish forces organized abroad. The traditions of the crownless eagle were revived in the leftist independence movement — in the units of the People's Guard and later of the People's Army, and in the Polish Army formed in the Soviet Union.

The Polish People's Republic adopted as its emblem the eagle without a crown. The poet Konstanty Ildefons Gałczyński very aptly rendered the sense of this decision when he wrote that the eagle "took off its crown to lay it at the feet of the people".

The Decree of 7 December 1955 on the emblem and colours of the Polish People's Republic approved the official effigy of the eagle as it appeared in the design of 1927 but deleting the crown. This design was also confirmed in a law passed on 31 January 1980 on the national emblem, anthem and colours of the Polish People's Republic.

The National Colours

Chronologically speaking, the second symbol of our state are its colours: white and red. On the flag, they assume the form of two horizontal bands of equal width, the upper white and the lower red. The origin of this symbol is related to the beginnings of the Piast eagle from which it is directly derived, the white and red colours being — in accordance with the principles of heraldry — an equivalent of the white eagle on a field of red, and constituting a synthesis of the emblem. The flags of other States and some municipal flags are related in like manner to the theme of the emblem.

While white and red were from the beginning the colours of our emblem, they had a long way to go until they appeared on the flag and were adopted as the national colours. The concept of the state flag and of the national colours belongs to modern states of the 18th and 19th centuries. The Polish national colours did not take final shape until the modern era, either. In earlier times, we find them on royal standards and military flags; however, they were not then state colours in the full sense of the term. The proper state flag represented a white eagle or the Eagle and Pursuit against a red background.

In the first half of the 18th century, white cockades were introduced on the caps of the Polish army, in the foreign fashion, as the distinctive sign of a soldier. The white of those cockades was the first colour in Poland to have symbolic significance — the sign of the Polish soldier.

White, however, was identified as the royal colour. It was used by foreign monarchs, e.g. in France, where it was supplanted by the tricolour of the French Revolution — blue, white and red. From the end of the 18th century onwards, radical social movements in Europe used the three-coloured cockade as the emblem of universal revolution. In Poland, these colours were worn by the radical Jacobins in the days of the Kościuszko Insurrection of 1794.

The Polish Legions, organized in the post-partition period in Italy under the command of General Jan Henryk Dąbrowski, retained the colours of the Polish uniform but used cockades like those worn by the French "as a nation that protects free people" and shoulder-straps in the colours of the Cisalpine Republic (green, white and red). The French tricolour cockades were also used in the Polish Legions fighting at Napoleon's side. The most durable, however, proved to be the white cockade of the Polish armies; it was retained in the armies of the Duchy of Warsaw and of the Kingdom of Poland.

It was only the Rising of 1830—31 that brought essential changes. In sympathy with the army which gave the first signal for the rising, the civilian population adopted white cockades. At the same time, members of the radical faction of the movement pinned on the tricolour cockades of revolution. There also appeared white-and-red cockades, derived from the colours of the emblem which was revived at that time. The lack of uniformity of all these signs induced the Seym to take the problem of the cockades in hand. On 7 February 1831, the resolution on the national white-and-red cockade was adopted. It was a resolution of major importance, being the first legally valid act adopted by the nation's supreme representatives to regulate the problem of the Polish colours in full accordance with tradition and the principles of heraldry. White and red formally became Poland's national colours.

After the defeat of the uprising, the white-and-red cockades — like other symbols — were severely forbidden by the tsarist authorities. The tradition of reverence for this sign was maintained in exile. The red-and-white cockade marked the presence of Poles wherever they fought "for our freedom and yours" — in Hungary and Italy, on the barricades of Paris, Vienna and Berlin. In Poland, it reappeared in all liberation movements and uprisings. White and red also appeared on Polish flags, both in exile and — during uprisings — in Poland, although the form and the arrangement of colours were not uniform. It was in those times that amaranth became the most popular hue of the red in national colours. This was not justified from the heraldic point of view, and amaranth — widely used in the 19th century — was later forsaken.

When the First World War brought hopes of regaining independence, the patriotic and national feelings of the Polish people manifested themselves through symbols — red-and-white flags, banners and standards. Warsaw was still under German occupation when, on 3 May 1916, a mass manifestation took place there to celebrate the 125th anniversary of the Constitution, with the demonstrators carrying Polish emblems and flags. On 11 November 1918, a Warsaw University student hung a big white-and-red flag on the Radziwiłł Palace, the seat of the German authorities; it heralded the approach of independence. The Second Commonwealth was being born in festive settings of white and red.

In 1919, the Seym of the reborn state adopted the official design of the flag — white and red — which has remained unchanged, to this day.

How great were the moral values associated with the national colours, became evident during the Second World War.

In the darkest days of Nazi enslavement, the white and red colours were the battle sign of all Poles. Prohibited under penalty of death, they appeared on the streets of Warsaw on national holidays — they gave comfort, aroused hope, gave people new heart; they were a challenge to the enemy. White-and-red arm-bands and badges were worn by Polish guerrillas and underground fighters on the uniforms taken from the enemy. In the days of the Warsaw Rising of 1944, national flags marked out the areas occupied by the insurgents — enclaves of hard-won and short-lived liberty. Polish soldiers fighting on nearly all fronts of the war marked their glorious battle trail with white-and-red flags. On 2 May 1945, a Polish soldier hoisted the white-and-red flag on the Prussian Victory Column in Berlin.

The National Anthem

The emblems and colours of many nations are derived from symbols whose origins go back to the Middle Ages. National anthems, on the other hand, are for the most part associated with the formation of modern nations. Such is also the case with the Polish anthem.

The Polish anthem, born in the modern era, had its predecessors — earlier national songs bearing the character of anthems. The oldest of them was the "ancestral song" (*carmen patrium*) or the *Bogurodzica* (The Mother of God) which was sung by Polish knights on the battlefields of Grunwald and Varna. In later times, however, up to the end of the 18th century, none of the soldiers' songs became a truly national song.

King Stanislaus Augustus in the 18th century was the first to call attention to the need for a national anthem. The poem by Ignacy Krasicki entitled *Święta miłości kochanej Ojczyzny* (O, Sacred love of the beloved Fatherland), written in 1774 for the Cadets' School in Warsaw, did not become generally accepted. In the Kościuszko Insurrection, the *Song of the National Cavalry*, to the tune of the French *Ça Ira*, was widely sung. There also arose at this time the soldiers' song *To Arms, Brothers, to Arms!* — to the tune of its contemporary, the *Marseillaise*, song of the French Revolution.

Modern national anthems originate from two different sources. Some came into being on the initiative of rulers or governments; they appealed to God to preserve the king and the monarchy. Others, like the *Marseillaise*, were born from the patriotic aspirations and outbursts of nations. Poland's national song, the Dąbrowski Mazurka — formerly known as *The Song of the Polish Legions* — belongs to this latter category.

This song was born in 1797, outside the frontiers of Poland, at the time of the formation by General Jan Henryk Dąbrowski of the Polish Legions attached to the French army in Italy. In an atmosphere of enthusiasm and hopes for a prompt return to Poland, it was written (to the tune of a popular mazurka) by Józef Wybicki, a distinguished leader and publicist of the patriotic camp. It was sung for the first time in July 1797 at Reggio Emilia where the Polish Legions were stationed. The simple, heart-moving lyrics and the familiar tune caught on and were soon widely accepted by the soldiers. The Song of the Legions soon reached the country and was received with sincere enthusiasm; in Poland, minor changes were introduced to the original text.

The extraordinary popularity of the song can be explained chiefly by its opening words: "Poland has not yet perished as long as we are alive". These words evoked the conviction that the nation might survive in spite of enslavement if the people retained their national consciousness and were ready to fight for independence. The remaining words of the anthem expressed faith in the nation's own strength ("What alien force took away from us, we will take back with our swords") and in the future victories of the Poles ("Bonaparte gave us a good example how to win"). The chorus ("March, march, Dąbrowski") repeated after every verse was a profession of faith on the part of the Polish emigrés in the possibility of realizing their chief aim: "to become reunited with the nation".

The Song of the Legions became at once the symbol of Poland's indestructibility and hope in her rebirth, a symbol rallying all Poles, with no distinction as to social rank, in the struggle for the nation's freedom. It was sung on particularly solemn and historic occasions. It resounded on the fields of insurrectionary battles and in street demonstrations. There also appeared occasional versions of the Song of the Legions as well as various other songs to the same tune. The original text was the most popular, however.

After the defeat of the November Rising, the Dąbrowski Mazurka was banned as a national, seditious song. Its popularity was spreading outside of the country, to Poles in exile and among other nations. As the song of freedom fighters, it won sympathy in liberal circles in Germany and Britain. The phrase "Poland has not yet perished", translated into various languages, became a declaration in favour of the freedom of all nations. One can therefore easily understand the popularity of the Mazurka, particularly among the Slav peoples united by common adversities. It was translated into Czech and Slovak, while its lyrics and music inspired the Pan-slav, Croatian and Lusatian anthems. The notes of our Mazurka may be heard in Yugoslavia's anthem even today.

In the years of the First World War, when hopes were rising for the rebirth of the Polish State, the Dąbrowski Mazurka was widely sung, along with other national songs, such as Alojzy Feliński's supplicatory song *God, who hath protected Poland*, Kornel Ujejski's chorale *In smoke and flames* and Maria Konopnicka's *The Oath*. After the regaining of independence, discussions took place as to which of these songs should become Poland's national anthem. These debates ended in the victory of the Dąbrowski Mazurka, which had the advantage over the other songs of close ties with the traditions of struggle for national liberation, and of spirited melody. In 1926, the Mazurka was officially recognized as the national anthem and has so remained until the present day.

The truths contained in the old Song of the Legions revived and proved their topicality most forcefully during the last war. The words regained their old meaning and the melody reminded us that the tones of the Mazurka had so many times already accompanied the struggles of Poles for freedom.

The Polish soldiers carried the national anthem to all battlefields — from the Norwegian fiords to the deserts of Libya, from Lenino to Berlin. In Poland, how often was this the last sound uttered, the last thought of millions of Poles put to death! It also played an important role by raising the spirits of the population groaning under the Nazi yoke.

*

The history of the emblem, colours and anthem of our country recalled above enables us to see the varying content with which successive generations have invested those symbols. Passed on from generation to generation in defiance of the bans imposed by the partitioning powers, they acquired an all-national value. They became associated with the liberation struggles of the Polish people and played a unifying role. Those symbols belong to the republican tradition in Poland's history and are bound up with the slogans of democracy and progress. We find in them today the same ideals that they proclaimed in the past: the free and independent existence of the Polish state and common effort in the national cause.

The design of the emblem, the colours and the state flag, as well as the words and music of the national anthem are contained in a law approved by the Seym on 31 January 1980 (*Dziennik Ustaw PRL* or *Government Gazette*, No. 7, 11 March 1980, item 18), which also states the conditions and circumstances when the above may be used.

Stefan Krzysztof Kuczyński

II. The History of Poland

LIST OF POLISH SOVEREIGNS

I. PIAST DYNASTY

Early Feudal Monarchy

c. 960—992 Mieszko I
 992—1025 Boleslaus I the Brave (crowned in 1025)
1025—1034 Mieszko II Lambert (crowned in 1025)
1034—1058 Casimir I the Restorer
1058—1079 Boleslaus II the Bold (crowned in 1076)
1079—1102 Ladislaus I Herman
1102—1107 Zbigniew and Boleslaus III the Wrymouth
1107—1138 Boleslaus III the Wrymouth

The Period of Feudal Disintegration
(dukes ruling in Cracow)

1138—1146 Ladislaus II the Exile
1146—1173 Boleslaus IV the Curly
1173—1177 Mieszko III the Old
1177—1194 Casimir II the Just
1194—1202 Mieszko III the Old
      1202 Ladislaus Spindleshanks
1202—1210 Leszek the White
1210—1211 Mieszko the Stumbling
1211—1227 Leszek the White
1227—1229 Ladislaus Spindleshanks
1229—1232 Conrad of Mazovia
1232—1238 Henry the Bearded
1238—1241 Henry the Pious
1241—1243 Conrad of Mazovia
1243—1279 Boleslaus the Chaste
1279—1288 Leszek the Black
1288—1290 Henry Probus
1290—1291 Przemysł II (King 1295—1296)
1291—1305 Wenceslas II
      King of Bohemia
      Premyslid dynasty
      (King of Poland from 1300)

United Polish Kingdom

1306—1333 Ladislaus I the Short (King from 1320)
1333—1370 Casimir III the Great, King*

II. ANGEVIN DYNASTY

1370—1382 Louis of Hungary
1383—1399 Jadwiga

III. JAGIELLON DYNASTY

1386—1434 Ladislaus II Jagiello
1434—1444 Ladislaus III of Varna
1447—1492 Casimir IV the Jagiellonian
1492—1501 John Albert
1501—1506 Alexander
1506—1548 Sigismund I the Old
1548—1572 Sigismund II Augustus

IV. ELECTORAL KINGS

1573—1574 Henry of Valois
1576—1586 Stephen Báthory
1587—1632 Sigismund III Vasa
1632—1648 Ladislaus IV Vasa
1648—1668 John II Casimir Vasa
1669—1673 Michael Korybut Wiśniowiecki
1674—1696 John III Sobieski
1697—1706 Augustus II the Strong (Wettin)
1704—1709 Stanislaus Leszczyński
1709—1733 Augustus II the Strong
1733—1736 Stanislaus Leszczyński
1733—1763 Augustus III (Wettin)
1764—1795 Stanislaus Augustus Poniatowski

---

* Kings of Poland from this point on.

Before the Emergence of the Polish State

The earliest traces of human settlement on Polish territory are to be found in the south. Remains of settlement of primitive man (Pithecanthropus), dating back to the middle pleistocene, i.e. the last inter-glacial age, have been discovered in the layers of loess at Piekary near Cracow, in the Dark Cave (Jaskinia Ciemna) in Ojców and in the Kaczawy foothills at Kondratówka. These early inhabitants of the Polish lands hunted herbivorous animals, especially reindeer which were numerous at this time. The severe and humid climate created an environment similar to the present border zone between the Siberian tundra and taiga. After the middle-Polish glacier receded about 50,000 years B.C. at the latest, the first settlements of Neanderthal man appeared and their remains are to be seen in caves near Zawiercie and Ojców and in the area of present-day Cracow. They were inhabited by hunting and food gathering groups numbering several score individuals each. During the glacial recession settlement by hunters of the Lower Paleolithic — similar in build to modern man — reached the north of Little Poland where there was a temperate climate which gradually expanded to the north. There the animals they hunted already included deer, bison and bear.

In the Mazovian sandhills we find evidence of hunting grounds dating back to about 14,000 B.C.

Later millennia brought a warmer climate and lower humidity. The vegetation changed and conditions improved for the development of primitive agriculture which by 4200 B.C. was already fairly universal. The inhabitants of these settlements created the culture of the Lower Stone Age (Neolithic). They lived mainly in the areas of loess and loess-like soils of southern Poland (Silesia, Little Poland and the Lublin region). Gradually settlement by farmers and animal breeders spread north, to the more fertile regions of Kuyawy and the vicinity of Pyrzyce in western Pomerania. In that period, human settlements formed enclaves in vast territories which were either scarcely populated or not populated at all. A few flint mines for making tools dating from that period have been discovered in Little Poland (Sandomierz region), the largest of them being the gallery mine at Krzemionki Opatowskie. Goods made of stone from this region and from quarries in Lower Silesia at the foot of Mount Ślęża spread all over the lowlands, reaching north-western Europe and the steppes of the Ukraine.

The first influence of the Bronze Age can be noted before 1500 B.C. From this period date numerous bronze treasure hoards, including bracelets, ear-rings and other jewellery, testifying to the wealth of their owners. Since Polish copper deposits seem not to have been exploited at that time, bronze objects must have been imported, mainly from present-day Slovakia and Hungary. Bronze tools appeared later, chiefly elaborately adorned axes and swords. From among the farmer-stock-breeders there emerged a stratum of warrior knights.

Some time about the 13th century B.C., we observe in the Polish lands traces of a leap forward in civilization connected with the peoples belonging to the Lusatian culture. This culture initially embraced Saxony, Lusatia and Great Poland and later spread to the east. Favourable climatic conditions made possible a growth in population connected with the development of agriculture. Between 700 and 300 B.C., the large forti-fied settlements or "castle towns" with ramparts made from chests filled with earth and stone, replaced the former disper-sed settlements. They were built in the period when Scythian and Scytho-Sarmatian peoples from the steppes of south-eastern Europe threatened the local tribes. Traces of fighting with the Scythians, e.g. Scythian arrowheads, have been found among the remains of ramparts and living quarters.

The period of the Lusatian culture is characterized also by a con-siderable development of crafts, especially wood working. The fortified settlement discovered in 1933 on the peninsula of Lake Biskupin in Great Poland consists of well-planned parallel streets with 105 houses.

The long period during which the Lusatian culture existed in the Polish lands helped to unify the material culture of the inhabi-tants of these settlements. Traces discovered by archaeologists of similarities between the culture of the Lusatian tribes and that of the ancient and early medieval inhabitants of Poland permit the supposition that Lusatian elements played a vital role in the formation of Slav culture.

At the turn of the 4th and 3rd centuries B.C., Celts settled in southern Silesia and western Little Poland, and their cultural influence spread over a considerable area of Polish territory. The Celts popularized technical innovations from the Mediter-ranean countries, and the widespread knowledge of metal-smelting in Poland is attributed to their influence. Large smelting centres in the Świętokrzyskie Mountains, Silesia and Cracow arose during this period, and an important production centre of pottery intended for sale was established in the Cracow area (Nowa Huta).

By this time it was the period of the influence of the Roman Empire, whose territory stretched as far north as the southern foothills of the Carpathians. The roads leading through the Carpathian passes and the Moravian Gate contributed to the spread of the products of Roman civilization, such as ornaments and utility objects. Roman merchants on their way to the southern coast of the Baltic in quest of amber crossed the Polish lands. One such route led via Kalisz (Calisia) in Great Poland, mentioned by Ptolemy, the celebrated Alexandrian astronomer, geographer and mathematician of the 2nd century A.D., in the introduction to his *Geography*.

Evidence of intensive trade contacts is also provided by numerous hoards of coins dating from the period of the Roman Empire (1st to 4th century A.D.). Their distribution makes it possible to determine the main regions of settlement in this period.

In the 2nd and 3rd centuries numerous Gothic tribes migrating from Pomerania to the Black Sea drifted through Polish territory. For a time they lived among the local population. Traces have also been found in southern Poland of a halt made by the Huns during the period of migrations (the grave of a Hunnish prince at Jakuszowice in Little Poland).

Larger tribal migrations took place towards the close of the period of antiquity, during the 5th and 6th centuries. At this time, the Slav inhabitants of the Polish lands were moving southwards in search of better and richer places to settle. They occupied the Bohemian Lowland and Moravia, and began to settle Pannonia and the area of what is now Austria, reaching as far as Carinthia, Slovenia, Croatia and Dalmatia. Slavonic tribes also expanded to the west and occupied territories formerly inhabited by the Polabians, a Germanic tribe, entered into Thuringia and Bavaria and penetrated deep into present-day Germany. In what is today Austria and Bavaria, Slavonic tribes began to settle the Alpine valleys which were then still sparsely exploited. At the same time the eastern Slavs migrated from the steppes on the Dniester and Dnieper to the Balkans.

The medieval landscape was dominated by forest. Thick primeval forests covered the southern regions near the mountains; and virgin forests were also to be found on the remaining boundaries enclosing the Polish lands. The densest forests were in the west and north-east, where they divided the western Slav lands from the territories inhabited by the Baltic Prussians. Settlement took place in fertile land suitable for agriculture and in wooded regions at the foot of the mountains in Little Poland and Silesia. Deciduous trees had the most significance; especially important were beech and oak trees, which supplied valuable wood for building as well as nuts and acorns, which served as animal fodder or, in lean years, even as food for man. Medieval livestock was half wild and grazed in forests. Pigs were no different from wild boars; cows were small as were horses which were especially prized.

Soil was ploughed by means of wooden implements, chiefly primitive ploughs with blades made of iron. Fields were created by burning down forests; when the soil was exhausted they were left fallow and fresh lands were brought under the plough. Given the relative scarcity of population, there was plenty of land. Farmsteads varied in size depending on the number of draught animals and able bodied persons available to work them. Such farms were owned both by peasants and by warriors. Before the Polish state emerged in the 10th century, a group of lords was distinguishable within the tribal community. Their wealth depended on their moveable property, especially the number of slaves, cattle and horses, and on better weapons, implements and jewellery.

From the period of Slavonic migrations to the south and west, the first castle towns began to appear, giving rise to the development of new political organizations, for the time being of a tribal character. A castle town, especially in the south, covered an area of about fifteen, and sometimes over twenty hectares. In times of danger they provided shelter for those who lived in local tribal settlements. They were focal points for the agricultural population. There were also a few craftsmen who produced mainly metal objects and pottery.

The members of these tribes were freemen, but there were also slaves who worked mostly as servants in patriarchal families. Polygamy was practised among the Slavs before the adoption of Christianity, but was limited to the wealthiest tribesmen who could have two and sometimes three or four wives.

Wealth and influence depended also on the size of household. For this reason families with a larger number of slaves, or of relations, were wealthier and had more influence. The division of work in the household put a heavier burden on women, who had to work in the farmyard, prepare and store food, grind corn in the quern, make clothes and bring up children. In this respect the adoption of Christianity did not change much. On the other hand men worked in the field and occupied themselves with bee-keeping, which was widespread in the Middle Ages, fishing and hunting. Men also concerned themselves with the education of boys, preparing them for farm work and, especially, teaching them the use of weapons for hunting and warfare.

Customs were connected with pagan beliefs and therefore the more important feasts were at the same time religious rites, which coincided with the rhythm of the seasons and the vegetation cycle. Of special importance were the feast of summer solstice, known at first as *Kupała* and later as *Sobótka*, the harvest home festival in autumn and the festival of the dead in spring. Each tribe had its own totem to which its members prayed and made offerings.

Holy places were initially far from human settlement, usually in old oak groves. Great importance was acquired by two holy mountains in southern Poland — Ślęża in Silesia and Łysiec, later called Święty Krzyż (Holy Cross), in Little Poland. Both dominated fertile and thickly settled regions. A pantheon of Slavonic gods had also begun to emerge, in which a special role was played by Perun, the lord of fire and thunderbolts, who is mentioned in sources concerning Ruthenia and Pomerania. Forests, lakes and rivers were inhabited by lesser divinities and spirits. New houses of worship were built in which offerings were made of food, flower wreaths and sometimes skulls of large beasts, including the aurochs, the largest of the forest denizens. Belief in an after-life existed and found expression in funeral rites, the most important being the cremation of the dead and the burying of the ashes under a mound. Family life was symbolized by the hearth and therefore after entering her new house the bride walked round the hearth and sat down by it thereby taking over the household. Also newly-borns were carried round the fire. Adolescent boys passed under the care of the menfolk. This was connected with a ceremonial rite during which a boy's hair was shorn, which it appears was connected with being given a name. At the beginning Slavonic names were individual and the custom of inherited names did not emerge until after Christianity was adopted. Girls wore their hair long and plaited. Married women covered their heads with white scarves.

The First Piast Monarchy

The 9th century saw an intensive development of Slav state organizations to the south of the Carpathians. Greater Moravia, which incorporated tribal duchies in Bohemia as well as Slavonic domains in the Pannonian Lowlands, was set up at this time and its influence on the southern Polish lands accelerated the emergence of a state organization among the tribe of the Vislane who lived in the vicinity of the upper Vistula. It was the Polane, who inhabited the regions known later as Great Poland, who were the predecessors of the oldest reigning dynasty in Poland, the Piasts.

The Polish lands were united by the Polane in the 10th century which also saw the emergence of states bordering on Poland: Bohemia, Hungary and Rus. The first historical ruler of Poland was Mieszko I*. Court tradition has handed down to us the names of three of his supposed predecessors, Siemovit, Lestko (Leszek) and Siemomysł (Ziemomysł). In or about 960 Mieszko I reigned over Great Poland, Kuyawy and the central Polish regions of Łęczyca and Sieradz, and it is quite probable that he also brought Mazovia under his sway. His influence reached as far as the mouth of the Vistula and he intended to extend his conquests to Western Pomerania.

In 965, Mieszko I established political relations with the Bohemians and married Dobrava, a Bohemian princess, a union which facilitated the acceptance of the western rite in 966. The conversion to Christianity was an important political decision which strengthened Poland's position in Europe and resulted in the consolidation of state power. As a Christian ruler, Mieszko found it easier to make wider political contacts and lay the organizational foundations of a proper medieval monarchy. In international relations, Poland's conversion to Christianity supplied an ideological justification for the wars against the pagan Pomeranian and Polabian tribes.

In the struggle for Western Pomerania, Mieszko came into con-

---

* See p. 22 for a complete list of Polish monarchs.

flict with the Empire. In 976 he repulsed an expedition by the Emperor Otto II, but had to agree to pay tribute on the recently acquired territories. He allied himself with the Saxons against the Veleti. Then, about 990, after severing political ties with the Bohemians, Mieszko united the tribes living in Silesia and Cracow, which for some time had been under the rule of the Premyslids.

In a matter of a few years, Mieszko extended his rule to the regions between the Odra and the Bug and from the Sudeten and Carpathian Mountains to the Baltic. Linguistic and cultural similarities, as well as the absence of obvious natural barriers, favoured the permanence of the union thus created. At the turn of the 10th and 11th centuries, references to Poland and the Poles appeared for the first time in the writings of foreign chroniclers, to whose ears came more accurate information about the land of the first Piasts.

Mieszko's eldest son, Boleslaus the Brave (also called the Great) continued this expansive policy. He helped the Bishop of Prague, Adalbert, to organize a mission to Prussia, where the latter suffered the death of a martyr. The Bishop, connected with influential circles in the Church and the Empire, had been a popular figure. He was buried in Gniezno. Shortly after the death of Saint Adalbert in the year 1000, the young Emperor Otto III made a solemn pilgrimage to the grave of his friend.

During the meeting which followed in Gniezno between the Emperor and Boleslaus the Brave, the creation of an archbishopric in that town and of several subordinate bishoprics was announced, as a result of which the Polish State obtained an expanded Church hierarchy. Earlier, Mieszko I had subordinated his state to the superior of the Western Church, the Bishop of Rome, or the Pope as he was called, in order to create a counterweight to the influence of the Empire. In 1000 particularly favourable circumstances caused the two highest dignitaries of medieval western Europe — the Pope and the Emperor — to help realize the plans of Boleslaus who in the political arena supported the universalist programme of Otto III. However the early death of the Emperor thwarted these plans.

In 1003, during the struggle for the succession to the throne, Boleslaus seized Lusatia and Bohemia, while his army, which supported the weaker candidate to the throne, the Margrave Ekkehard, occupied Bavaria. This opened a long period of war between Poland and the Empire which lasted — in three stages

— from 1003 to 1018 and which revealed to the full Boleslaus' military and political genius. Although he failed to keep Bohemia under his rule, he appeared as the most powerful of the western Slav rulers. After signing the peace of Budziszyn (Bautzen) in 1018, he immediately embarked on an expedition against Rus and placed his son-in-law, Svyatopolk on the throne of Kiev.

Towards the end of Boleslaus' rule, the young Polish state attained its greatest significance, and shortly before his death Boleslaus had himself crowned King (1025) which at that time gave a ruler rights recognized in the whole of Europe.

The adoption of Christianity opened up Poland to the heritage of the culture of antiquity and the achievements of early medieval culture. This was made possible both through the acquisition of the art of writing, which was cultivated above all by the clergy, and by the establishment of contacts with the contemporary centres of cultural and artistic life. Foreign craftsmen built the stone walls of cathedrals and royal residences in such major towns as Gniezno, Poznań and Cracow. One foreign author, St. Bruno of Querfurt, wrote a memorial which justified Boleslaus' policy during the period of war with the Empire. Thus Poland's emergence into the broader political arena took place not only by force of arms. The ability to muster arguments through the use of the written word also existed.

The 10th and early 11th centuries saw the emergence of Poland's oldest towns. They accelerated the economic and social differences in Poland which from the time of the first Piasts assumed the character of an oligarchic monarchy governed by the ruler and a small group of lords. The latter had their own courts and, when necessary, their own bands of armed retainers. At that time, however, landed estates were poorly developed and the lords derived a considerable part of their incomes from running state institutions.

In the 11th century, the country united by the first Piasts was troubled by marked separatist tendencies. The people were not always happy with the ducal dignitaries and officials who had been set over them, and had a reluctant attitude towards the clergy which strove to impose on them new ethical patterns and customs differing from those they had known. Places of pagan worship were liquidated and the most famous were replaced by Christian churches. The Church attempted to endow many of the pagan rites and festivals with a Christian character.

However the christianization of traditional customs took time and lasted several centuries.

The application of particularly drastic measures contributed to the emergence of anti-Christian movements in the 1030's. Separatist tendencies, especially in Mazovia, gained ground. In 1038 or 1039, the unheralded invasion of Great Poland by Bretislaus of Bohemia resulted in the pillaging of the country's principal centres, including Gniezno and Poznań. Silesia was temporarily seized by the Bohemians, while the loss of Pomerania cut Poland off from the Baltic. The reconstruction of the weakened state was undertaken in Little Poland after the seat of power had been transferred from the Polanian centres to Cracow, this town being more closely connected with the centres of political life in western and eastern Europe.

The reigns of Casimir the Restorer and his son, Boleslaus the Bold, were a period of internal reorganization and reform of the organizational and economic basis of the monarchy. According to contemporary political doctrine, the ruler was overlord of the whole country and all its inhabitants, who are estimated to have numbered about one million. The free and unfree population was subordinated to stewards appointed by the prince or monarch, and to whom they paid tribute in kind, while specially appointed menials and craftsmen, who lived mostly in rural settlements, were obliged to work in the castle towns and princely courts and to guard the monarch's herds and protect the game, especially beavers, aurochs, bears and deer, which was reserved for the lords. The lords also reserved for themselves the fishing in the major rivers and lakes.

In the dispute between the Emperor Henry IV and Pope Gregory VII Hildebrand over the investiture, Boleslaus the Bold supported the Pope. In the presence of papal legates, he was crowned king in the rebuilt Gniezno cathedral in 1076. Despite his successes in foreign policy (his victorious expedition to Kiev) and internal affairs, he came into conflict with a group of nobles who resented his strong-arm method of ruling. The death sentence imposed on Bishop Stanislaus of Cracow in 1079 inflamed the situation, and the king had to flee to Hungary. During the reign of his younger brother, Ladislaus Herman, the influence of the powerful nobles at court increased.

Herman's son, Boleslaus III Wrymouth, largely restricted the power of the nobles. He gained the full support of the country after driving his elder brother, Zbigniew, from Poland and

1. Ferdynand Ruszczyc, *Soil*
Our native soil, the part of the continent we live in, has been impregnated with blood and sweat of many generations, for work and struggle have gone into the making of the thousand year old history of the Polish nation

2. Aleksander Lesser,
Death of Wanda
The history of each nation
opens with legend, with
fairy-tales of heroes who
fought mysterious ogres
and established early ci-
ties. The legend of Krak
and his daughter Wanda,
who refused to marry
a German prince and
flung herself into the
waves of the Vistula in-
stead, is one of the most
popular in Poland and
as every legend contains
a grain of truth, being
at the same time proof of
an early origin of Polish-
German conflicts

3. Korneli Szlegel,
Pilgrims Visiting Piast
According to another le-
gend, recorded by Gallus
Anonymus (12th cent.),
the author of Poland's
oldest chronicle, Polish
kings were descended
from peasants, the simple
wheelwright Piast, fol-
lowed by Siemovit, Lesko
and Siemomysl, and final-
ly Mieszko I, the first historic ruler of Poland.
Such were the origins of
the first royal house in
Poland which ruled until
the 14 th century and from
the 18th century on has
been called the Piast dy-
nasty. The angels in Szlegel's picture have been
sent to Piast's house to
announce the mission this
simple and honest pea-
sant has been entrusted by
Providence

4. Jan Matejko, *Introduction of Christianity in Poland*
By accepting the western rite in 966 Mieszko I brought Poland into the orbit of western culture, strengthened the position of the young state in Europe and averted the threat of German invasions which were always undertaken in the name of converting pagan tribes to Christianity.

5. Michał Bylina, *Boleslaus the Brave's Retainers on the Baltic*
Boleslaus (I) the Brave (reigned 992—1025), son of Mieszko I and the second ruler of Poland, was a clever politician of European standing who in his numerous victorious wars against the Empire established and consolidated the frontiers of his state in the west and also carried out conquests in the east

6. Piotr Michałowski, *Boleslaus the Brave's Entry into Kiev*

7. The historic development of the state emblem of Poland (1) Eagle on Boleslaus the Brave's denarius (early 11th cent.); (2) Eagle on Casimir the Just's coin (late 12th cent.); (3) Eagle on the shield of Duke Casimir of Opole (1222); (4) Eagle on the shield of Duke Henry V of Legnica (1289); (5) Eagle of Przemysł II (1295); (6) Eagle on the tomb of Henry (IV) Probus (early 14th cent.); (7) Eagle on the coronation sword of Polish kings (1320); (8) Casimir the Great's eagle; (9) Ladislaus Jagiello's eagle; (10) Casimir the Jagiellonian's eagle; (11) Sigismund I's eagle; (12) Sigismund Augustus' eagle; (13) State emblem from the Jagiellon period; (14) Stephen Báthory's eagle; (15) State emblem from the Stephen Báthory period; (16) Eagle from the Vasa period; (17) State emblem from the Sigismund III period; (18) John III's eagle; (19) State emblem from the period of Augustus II and Augustus III; (20) State emblem from the Stanislaus Augustus period; (21) Stanislaus Augustus' eagle; (22) Eagle on a regimental banner (1807); (23) Emblem of the Duchy of Warsaw (1807—15), (24) Emblem from the November Insurrection (1831); (25) Emblem of the Kingdom of Poland (1842 design); (26) Eagle on the banner of the Polish Legion in Hungary (1848); (27) Emblem from the January Insur-

rection (1863); (28) Emblem of the Polish Republic (1919—27); (29) Emblem of the Polish Republic (1927—45); (30) Emblem of the Polish People's Republic

4

5

6

10

11

12

16

17

18

22

23

24

28

29

30

8,9. *The Legend of St. Hedvig of Silesia*
The battle of Legnica (1241), in which the Polish army suffered defeat and Duke Henry (II) the Pious of the Silesian Piast dynasty was killed, held back the Tartar invasion of Europe. The picture from the medieval *Legend of St. Hedvig of Silesia* shows the Tartars taking the severed head of the duke impaled on a spear round the walls of the city besieged by Tartar hordes

Hic fert caput einste duas henna filij sce hedwis i lancea acharris ante castrum legnicz

Hic redit in sympnis bea hedwigis annmā filij siu duas henna ducencem ab angelis in paradysum

10. Jan Matejko, *Ladislaus the Short Breaking off Negotiations with John of Lizemburg, Grand Master of the Teutonic Order, during a Congress in Brześć Kujawski*
The reign of Ladislaus the Short (1296—1333) saw the unification of the Polish state after 180 years of feudal disintegration. It was also a period of protracted wars against the Teutonic Order, crowned with the first victory at Płowce in 1331. The picture shows an episode of this Polish-German conflict

11. Wojciech Gerson, *Casimir the Great and Jews*

Jews, who were brought to Poland by Casimir the Great (1333—70), played an important role in the history of Poland. This old people with its rich cultural, heritage in time took root in Poland and repeatedly demonstrated its attachment to the Polish state which they defended together with Poles against enemies and invaders

12. Jan Matejko, *The Battle of Grunwald* (detail)
On 15 July 1410 the combined armies of Poland, Lithuania and Ruthenia, under the command of King Ladislaus Jagiello, gained an overwhelming victory over the Teutonic Knights. Jan Matejko's portrayal of this greatest battle of the Middle Ages is a masterpiece of battle painting

13. Marcello Bacciarelli, *Ladislaus Jagiello Granting Privileges to the Cracow Academy*
Founded in 1364 by Casimir the Great and revived in 1400 by Ladislaus Jagiello and Jadwiga, in the 15th and 16th centuries the Cracow Academy, the oldest higher education institution in Poland known from the mid-19th century on as the Jagiellonian University, was famous for its high standards of scholarship and its outstanding graduates, including Nicolaus Copernicus and Andrzej Frycz-Modrzewski

14, 15. *Balthasar Behem's Code* (details)
Written down in 1505 by Balthasar Behem, Cracow scribe, the Code is a collection of guild statutes. It also contains 27 colour pictures depicting life in old Cracow towards the end of the Middle Ages and at the beginning of the Renaissance, including a view of a street with stallkeepers and interior of a tailor's shop

16. *The Pontifical of Erazm Ciołek*
The Pontifical of Erazm Ciołek, Bishop of Płock, which dates from 1515, is an equally sumptuous book and its illustrations show court life and grand ceremonies, such as the bishop's
investiture, pontifical mass and royal coronation, the last one reproduced here

17. Łukasz Evert, *Triumphal March of Casimir the Jagiellonian after the Capture of Malbork*. During the reign of Casimir the Jagiellonian Prussian towns, including Gdańsk and Toruń, formed a confederation against the Teutonic Order. This resulted in the outbreak of what came to be known as the Thirteen Years' War (1454—66) and eventually Poland recovering Gdańsk Pomerania, Michałów and Chełmno regions, Warmia, Elbląg and Malbork. The frieze from the Gdańsk town hall shows an episode from this war

18. Marcello Bacciarelli, *The Prussian Homage*
The question of the Teutonic Order was finally resolved in 1525 when, with the consent of
Poland, a secular Prussian Duchy was formed (in the 18th century it would become one of
the invaders of Poland) and the Grand Master Albert Hohenzollern, who became a duke
owing fealty to the Polish king, paid homage to Sigismund I at the Cracow marketplace

19. Anonymous, *The Battle of Orsza*
In the 16th century Poland, joined with Lithuania on the basis of a personal union, engaged
in the latter's war against Muscovy, the object being recovery of the Ruthenian territory

which had previously belonged to Lithuania. This oldest battlepiece in the history of Polish painting depicts the victorious battle of Orsza fought by the Polish—Lithuanian armies under Konstanty Ostrogski in 1514

20. Jan Matejko, *The Raising of the Sigismund Bell into a Tower of the Cathedral in Cracow in 1521.*
The Renaissance, known in Poland as the Golden Age, came to Poland during the reign of Sigismund (I) the Old (1506—48) and his son Sigismund (II) Augustus (1548—72) and brought a great flowering of art and learning. The picture shows the ceremony of raising the famous Sigismund Bell into a tower of the Wawel Cathedral, in the presence of Sigismund the Old, his spouse, Queen Bona, son Sigismund Augustus and retinue

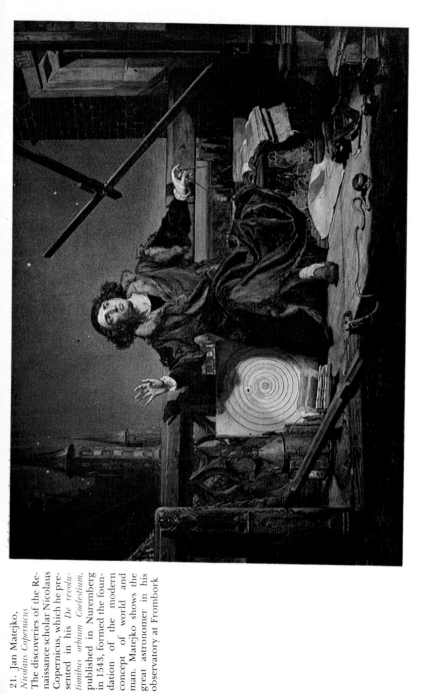

21. Jan Matejko,
Nicolaus Copernicus

The discoveries of the Renaissance scholar Nicolaus
Copernicus, which he pre-
sented in his *De revolu-
tionibus orbium Coelestium*,
published in Nuremberg
in 1543, formed the foun-
dation of the modern
concept of world and
man. Matejko shows the
great astronomer in his
observatory at Frombork

22. Isaak van dem Blocke, *Allegory of the Union of Gdańsk with Poland*
Executed in 1608 on the ceiling of a room in the Gdańsk town hall,
this painting attests to the close links between this Baltic port and the
rest of the country. One of the oval medallions depicts Mercury,
the god of commerce, giving his blessing to the exchange of goods
of the earth (Ceres, or Poland) and the sea (Neptune, symbolizing
Gdańsk)

23. Jan Krieg, *A Panorama of Gdańsk*
Gdańsk, a port situated on the Baltic at the mouth of the Vistula,
played an important role in grain trade. During the Vasa period
(17th cent.) it was a flourishing cultural centre

24. Bernardo Belotto, called Canaletto, *The Arrival of Jerzy Ossoliński at Rome in 1633*

The ceremonious entry into Rome in 1633 of Jerzy Ossoliński, Grand Chancellor of the Crown and adviser to Ladislaus IV, whom the king sent as an envoy to the Pope Urban VIII, was a sumptuous display of the rich variety of Polish customs which was intended to dazzle Europe. This was perhaps the most magnificent event in the history of Polish diplomacy and as such has been often recorded in painting

25. Witold Piwnicki,
Żółkiewski at Cecora

The 17th century saw
protracted wars against
Sweden, Muscovy,
the Tartars, Turks,
Hungarians and Cos-
sacks. In September
1620 the Polish army
was completely rou-
ted by the Turks at
Cecora, one of the
most disastrous battles
in the history of Po-
land in which Stani-
sław Żółkiewski, the
Grand Hetman of the
Crown, was killed

STA VIATOR ET CONSIDERA, QVOMODO INFIRMA MVNDI, ELEGIT
DEVS, VT CONFVNDAT FORTIA. 12000 SVECORVM CVM MILLERO
DVCE HIC OPPVGNAVERE PAVLINAM SOBOLEM, AST PRÆTER
DEDECVS REPORTAVERE NIHIL, DOMINO DEO EXERCITVVM
MANVS NOSTRAS DOCENTE AD PRÆLIVM ET DIGITOS NOSTR.
AD BELLVM THAVMATVRGA MATRE ET S. PATRE NOSTRO
PRIMO EREMITA, S. IOANNE EVANGELISTA TOTAQVE CÆLESTI
CVRIA PRO NOBIS MANIFESTE STANTE, IN SIGNIS ET POR-
TENTIS. ANNO 1655 PORTENSVM 1655 MORTE SVA...

26. Anonymous, *The Siege of the Jasna Góra Monastery*
The Swedish invasion of 1655—60 provoked opposition of the entire nation, particularly
after the successful defence of the Paulite Monastery at Jasna Góra in Częstochowa. The siege of the monastery has been taken up by many artists, including the writer Henryk Sienkiewicz and the painter of this picture, an obscure monk who was an eyewitness to those events

27. Leopold Loeffler, *Czarniecki's Death*
The hero of the war against Sweden in 1655 was Stefan Czarniecki, the Field Hetman of the Crown, who at the head of the national movement of gentry and peasants liberated the country from the Swedish "deluge". Loeffler's romantic picture shows the hero's death, his parting with his horse, his faithful companion

28. Józef Brandt, *John III Sobieski Departing from Wilanów*
John III Sobieski (1674—96), the victor in the famous battle of Christian Europe against Turks in 1683, was married to Marie-Casimire d'Arquien ("Marysieńka") of France. His magnificent court at Wilanów near Warsaw represented a mixture of western culture with elements of eastern customs acquired during his Turkish wars. Brandt conveys a picture of the Baroque sumptuousness of John III's court

29. Anonymous, *The Battle of Vienna*
The Relief of Vienna (1683), in which the combined Polish, Austrian and German armies under the command of John III completely routed the Turkish army, put an end to Turkish expansion in Europe

30. Anonymous, *Free Election at Wola near Warsaw*

After the last Jagiellon, Sigismund Augustus, died without issue in 1572, Polish kings began to be elected in so-called free elections at a diet of the entire gentry which usually took place at Wola near Warsaw. At the election field the gentry were grouped according to voivodships while the Senate, which considered the latter's votes, occupied the central position

31. Bernardo Belotto called Canaletto, *Krakowskie Przedmieście Street in Warsaw*
This Italian painter who worked in Poland in 1767—80 painted a series of Warsaw views
from the period of the last king of Poland, Stanislaus Augustus. His town-scapes executed
with photographic accuracy proved helpful when Warsaw was being reconstructed following
the Second World War

32. Bernardo Belotto, called Canaletto, *Długa Street in Warsaw*

34. Kazimierz Wojniakowski, *The Passing of the Constitution of May Third*
One of the last attempts at rescuing the motherland was a progressive constitution, known as the Constitution of May Third, which was drawn up by a group of enlightened Poles and passed on 3 May 1791 by the Great Seym. This second constitution in the world — after that of the United States — formulated principles of government in Poland. Soon, however, it was abolished by the treacherous Conferederation of Targowica. The passing of the constitution in the Warsaw Castle has been depicted by many painters, including Kazimierz Wojniakowski, who was connected with the progressive camp of reform

33. Jan Matejko, *Rejtan*
In the second half of the 18th century, Prussia, Austria and Russia took advantage of Poland being weakened by protracted wars and carried out the first partition. Jan Matejko's famous picture shows Tadeusz Rejtan, deputy from the Novogrod region, barring with his own body the way to the chamber where the Seym marshal and senators would sign the infamous treaty of partition

35. Stanisław Batowski-Kaczor, *The Battle of Savannah*

In this period many Poles fought for the freedom of other peoples. Among them were Thaddeus Kościuszko, military engineer and graduate of the Knights' School, and Colonel Casimir Pulaski, both of them heroes of the American War of Independence. The latter was killed in 1779 in the battle of Savannah

36. Michał Stachowicz, *Thaddeus Kosciuszko Taking an Oath of Allegiance in the Marketplace in Cracow*

After the abolishment of the Constitution of May Third and the second partition carried out by Prussia and Russia, a national insurrection with Thaddeus Kosciuszko as Supreme Commander broke out in Poland. The insurrection found many supporters among the peasants who were promised abolishment of serfdom and lowering of labour dues

38. Aleksander Orłowski, *Slaughter of Praga in Warsaw*
The capture on 4 November 1794 of Praga, the right bank suburb of Warsaw, by Russian troops under General Suvorov spelt an end to the Kosciuszko Insurrection. Aleksander Orłowski depicts the slaughtering of the civilian population of this part of Warsaw

37. Aleksander Orłowski, *The Battle of Racławice*
From his own studies made on the spot, Aleksander Orłowski, a participant of the Kosciuszko Insurrection, painted the familiar representation of the battle of Racławice fought on 4 April 1794, including the conclusive charge of peasant scythebearers on Russian guns

39. Marcello Bacciarelli, *Napoleon Granting the Constitution to the Duchy of Warsaw*
Poles organized detachments fighting at the side of Napoleon against Austria, Prussia and then Russia. Following his lightning victory over Prussia and the entry of the French army to Warsaw, Napoleon formed the Duchy of Warsaw from part of the Polish territory and on 22 July 1807 granted it a constitution modelled on the French one

40. Henryk Pillati, *Death of Berek Yoselevich at Kock*

Colonel Berek Joselevich, a Jewish merchant, organized a Jewish cavalry regiment during the Kosciuszko Insurrection in 1794 and as a soldier in the army of the Duchy of Warsaw was killed in 1807 during the battle of Kock

41. Piotr Michałowski, *The Battle of Somosierra*
Polish soldiers took part in many campaigns during the Napoleonic wars, some of them contrary to Polish interests. Piotr Michałowski, Poland's most outstanding Romantic painter, rendered a daring charge of the Polish light cavalry at Somosierra in Spain in 1808

42. January Sucho-
dolski, *The Death of
Cyprian Godebski at
Raszyn*

In 1809, during the
war with Napoleon,
Austrian troops en-
tered the Duchy of
Warsaw and pro-
ceeded in the direc-
tion of the capital.
During the heroic
defensive battle at
Raszyn, in which the
Polish army was com-
manded by Prince
Joseph Poniatowski,
nephew of the last
king of Poland, the
poet Cyprian Godeb-
ski was killed

43. Jan Nepomucen Bizański, *The Raising of the Kosciuszko Mound in Cracow*

This picture is a review of the Cracow community which in 1821 raised this characteristic monument in honour of Thaddeus Kosciuszko. In the period of national subjection many similar ceremonies were held, the purpose being the commemoration of important anniversaries and the paying of tribute to national heroes among whom Kościuszko occupied a chief place next to Prince Joseph Poniatowski

44. Anonymous, after Horace Vernet, *Death of Prince Joseph Poniatowski*

The death of Prince Poniatowski in the waters of the Elster during the Battle of the Nations at Leipzig is enveloped in Romantic legend which, owing to many literary descriptions and paintings, produced a vision of a national hero who, like his ancient predecessors, is ready to sacrifice his life for his motherland

45. Wincenty Kasprzycki, *Fine Art Exhibition in Warsaw in 1828*

The Congress of Vienna in 1815, which introduced a new division of Europe, formed from part of the Polish territory the Kingdom of Poland joined by a personal union with Russia. Initially the Tsar Alexander conducted a liberal policy which favoured the development of industry, education and culture

46. Marcin Zaleski
The Capture of the Arsenal

On 29 November, the famous November night, when conspirators from Warsaw's Infantry Officers' School under Piotr Wysocki, supported by the Warsaw populace and students, occupied key positions in the city, the insurrection of 1830—31 broke out. The capture of the Arsenal was one of the major episodes during the November night

47. Wojciech Kossak,
The Battle of Olszynka Grochowska

The battle at Grochów near Warsaw, fought on 25 February 1831, was one of the hardest and most bloody battles during the whole of the November Insurrection

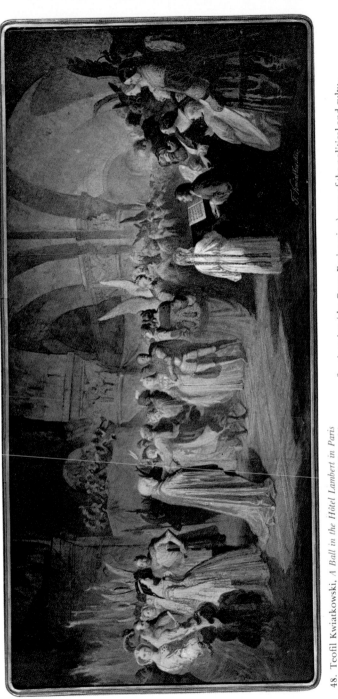

48. Teofil Kwiatkowski, *A Ball in the Hôtel Lambert in Paris*
The collapse of the November Insurrection was followed by a wave of emigration (the Great Emigration), one of the political and cultural centres of which was the Hôtel Lambert in Paris. In his series of paintings entitled *A Ball in the Hôtel Lambert* or *Chopin Polonaise*, the emigré painter Teofil Kwiatkowski shows a gathering of Poles, including Prince Adam Czartoryski, Adam Mickiewicz and Frédéric Chopin, as well as various figures in historical dress, for example hussars, performing a strange, half-dreamy dance to the tunes of a Chopin mazurka

49. Michał Stachowicz, *Harvest-home Festival*
19th century artists were fond of picturesque folk dress and customs and an idyllic picture of the countryside. One of them was Michał Stachowicz who painted an ideal picture of coexistence of the village and the court

50. Anonymous, *The Galician Slaughter of 1846*
A different picture of the countryside is offered by the painter of The Galician Slaughter, or the peasant uprising in the Austrian-occupied part of Poland in 1846, when peasants under Jakub Szela turned against landlords in their struggle for abolishment of serfdom

51. Artur Grottger, *Farewell to an Insurgent*
Artur Grottger's *Farewell to an Insurgent* and *Welcome to an Insurgent* show the woman as
a personification of Poland who, giving priority to the welfare of her nation over her own,
sends her beloved man to battle and, when he returns defeated, accords him a cool welcome
as if reproachful that he has failed in his duty

52. Artur Grottger, *Welcome to an Insurgent*

53. Jan Matejko, *Poland Enfettered*
Of all the 19th century uprisings — the November Insurrection of 1830—31, the Cracow
Revolution of 1846, and the Great Poland Uprising of 1848 — the most disastrous and
bloody was the January Insurrection of 1863—64. Matejko's allegory is an allusion to the
collapse of the January Insurrection and depicts the tsarist executioners putting the Polish
nation in irons

54. Jacek Malczewski, *On the Etape*

The ordeal of exiles in Siberia, of those who were sent there following the collapse of the January Insurrection and in other circumstances, was best depicted by Jacek Malczewski whose picture expresses both the helplessness of defeat and the germs of a new rebellion

55. Jacek Malczewski, *Melancholy*
This picture embodies all aspects of the 19th century in Poland, the one hundred years of national subjection and liberation struggles, the fresh romanticism of youthful outbursts, the bitter despair of defeat and the senile impotence of the close of a century

56. Aleksander Gierymski, *Sand-diggers*
In the second half of the 19th century, the life of the rural and town proletariat began to win
interest of writers and artists whose approach to the situation of workers and peasants was
often critical

57. Kazimierz Alchimowicz, *Hire of Farm Hands*

58. Stanisław Lentz, *Strike*
The underprivileged gradually grew conscious of social injustice and a workers' movement was born. The first Polish workers' party, the Proletariat, was established in 1882 and a wave of strikes swept over Poland in 1905

59. Michał Bylina, *The Red Regiment of Warsaw*
During the First World War and the Russian Revolution prospects for the restoration of independence became real. The latter was actively supported by many Poles

60. Stanisław Bagieński
*The Disarming of Germans
in Warsaw*
Not only Piłsudski's Legions and Polish soldiers in the Russian Revolution fought for Polish independence. Taking advantage of the internal difficulties of the partitioning powers, the civilian population proceeded to disarm foreign soldiers and expel occupation authorities without assistance from abroad

61. Michał Bylina, *September 1939*
After twenty years of peaceful reconstruction and unification of the country, which for 123 years had been divided into three partition zones, Hitler's armies attacked Poland on 1 September 1939. Throughout September the Polish army put up heroic resistance to the overwhelming enemy forces. This was the beginning of the long struggle conducted by Poles on all fronts of the Second World War

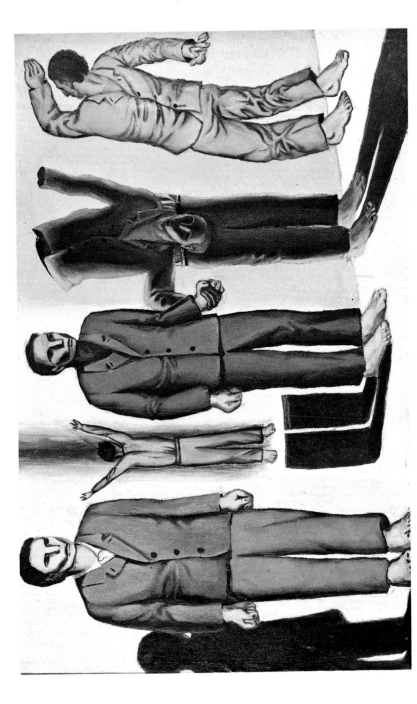

62. Andrzej Wróblewski, *Firing Squad*
The Nazis subjected Poles to extraordinarily brutal terror. Street round-ups and executions constituted an everyday occurrence during the occupation

63. Jerzy Krawczyk, *A Worthless Cargo*
This is a metaphorical picture of the trial of the Jewish nation sentenced by Nazism to total annihilation. In the concentration camps established by the Nazis in Poland millions of people of all nationalities perished

64. Andrzej Wróblewski, *Partisans*

Poles fought against the Nazis on all fronts, in east and and west, and above all inside the country, in the underground movement organized by the Home Army, the People's Army and the Peasant Battalions which waged a real war against the invaders

65. Stanisław Poznański, *Soldiers of the Kosciuszko Division Taking an Oath*
The First Tadeusz Kościuszko Infantry Division, formed in the Soviet Union, soon grew into the First Polish Army which took part in the liberation of Poland and the storming of Berlin

66. Michał Bylina, *The Battle of Lenino*
Lenino, on 12 and 13 October 1943, was the first battle fought by the First Division at the side of the Red Army

67. Stefan Garwatowski, *Hill 593*
This picture shows the II Polish Corps in the bloody storming of the German-occupied monastery at Monte Cassino in Italy in May 1944

68. Marcin Szczerba, *A Dying City*
The Warsaw Uprising, which lasted from 1 August to 2 October 1944 brought the
death of 16,000 insurgents and 150,000 civilians; 25,000 insurgents were wounded, 75
per cent of the city was completely demolished following the capitulation

69. Aleksander Kobzdej, *Pass Me a Brick*
After the liberation the people, fired by sincere enthusiasm, set to reconstructing the country. Later on the situation was different and there were also changes in art which turned to socialist realism employing stereotype views of life detached from reality

71. Juliusz Krajewski, *Land for the Peasants*

Nationalization of industry and agrarian reform formed the foundation of the new, socialist system in Poland. These early beginnings of the important political and social changes were often dealt with in the socialist realist painting of the 1950s

70. Helena Krajewska, *A Youth Brigade Breaking a Record on the Building Site*

72. Andrzej Feliks Szumigaj, *Worker's Head*

The leading force in post-war Poland has been the working class which gradually has become increasingly conscious of its role of the real master of its motherland responsible for her development and full sovereignty

defeating an expedition led by the Emperor Henry V. After securing his southern frontier with Bohemia, Boleslaus began an intensive campaign to conquer Pomerania, which had been separated from Poland during the period of anarchy following the death of Boleslaus the Brave. The conquest and annexation of Gdańsk Pomerania was crowned by his victory at Nakło in 1113. In 1122, Boleslaus Wrymouth subdued Warcislaus I, the ruler of Western Pomerania.

Foreign successes helped to make possible the reorganization of internal relations. In the face of the growing influence of the secular lords, Boleslaus Wrymouth courted the Church in order to gain support for his policies.

The Period of Division

Before his death in 1138, Boleslaus Wrymouth attempted to forestall the internal struggles which could result if antagonisms between his sons were aggravated by the intervention of various quarrelling magnate factions. For this reason he established the principle of seniority, by which the younger sons were to rule over separate districts, while the oldest brother, the "senior", was to be the sovereign prince who decided on all matters of foreign policy and Church affairs throughout the entire kingdom. Apart from his own inheritance, the senior was to receive the most important centres of Cracow, Gniezno and Pomerania. In order to limit the possibility of any kind of intervention on the part of the Empire, the court had this statute recognized by the Roman curia. However, the following years were to show up the instability of this system.

As Boleslaus' sons, backed by various groups of nobles, struggled for power, the internal divisions became well established. Gradually separate dukedoms emerged, each with its own court and official hierarchy.

After the defeat of the first senior prince, Ladislaus II called the Exile (1146), Boleslaus the Curly assumed power. Although at first he resisted Imperial intervention, he was unable to repel an expedition by Frederick Barbarossa in 1157. Though forced to pay homage, he managed to keep the country unified. Later, especially after the death of Boleslaus the Curly in 1173, centrifugal tendencies increased and led to a perpetuation of the divisions which were also characteristic of other countries in central and eastern Europe at that time. Even the authoritarian Mieszko the Old (d. 1202) could not prevent the weakening of the senior prince's power. District duchies assured local nobles of wider access to the government.

In the Poland of the 12th century a development of cultural life can be observed, which found expression in artistic and intellectual activity but above all in a change of manners. As early as the second half of the 11th century, the influence of chivalry was evident at the royal court and shortly spread to the leading families. The sons of nobles received the names of legendary heroes, especially those of the Trojan War. Names such as Hector and Ajax were popular in Poland at this time. The oldest Polish chronicle written at the beginning of the 12th century by an anonymous foreigner, later known as Gallus Anonymus, is saturated with the spirit of chivalrous legends. It represents the views held in court circles and justifies Boleslaus Wrymouth's laws, and is thus an early specimen of political writing which was read and commented on by both nobles and clergy.

At the end of the 11th century and during the reign of Boleslaus Wrymouth, the royal court was a lively centre concerned with cultural development which it promoted by inviting educated foreigners, especially clerics, who later spread word of Poland in Europe. At the Sicilian court of Roger II, the geographer Al-Idrisi characterized mid-12th century Poland as a land of wise and learned men, versed in Latin, who came from various parts of the world.

Feudal comminution limited the court's role in intellectual life. We note, however, a rise in the significance of the Church and of cathedral schools in Cracow, Płock and Wrocław. The activities of Bishops Alexander and Walter of Mallonne in Wallonia was of major significance. Many foreign artists, among them painters and sculptors who decorated the basilicas of Romanesque cathedrals, collegiate churches and monasteries, also came to Poland at this time. Romanesque sculptures in the Benedictine Abbey in Ołbin near Wrocław and in the church in Czerwińsk in Mazovia, reveal the hand of Italian masters. Romanesque chapels built in smaller castle towns and even in country gentlemen's residences (Skalbmierz, Prandocin and Jędrzejów) frequently achieve a high artistic standard. In this way the influence of art gradually began to spread out to the countryside, which at this time also began to enjoy the products of the craftsmen who gathered in the embryonic towns.

In the 13th century, feudal disintegration became even more serious. The duchies inherited by the Piast rulers were re-divided and re-united. The reigning house was divided into several branches ruling over Little Poland, Great Poland, Lower and Upper Silesia and the Kuyawy-Łęczyca region. The local dynasty of King Warcislaus I, who owed allegiance to Boleslaus Wrymouth, ruled over divided Western Pomerania. In Gdańsk Pomerania, one of the governors general of Sobieslaus I set up his own dynasty, which also divided this region into even smaller duchies.

In 1177 Casimir the Just seized power, which was an infringement of the principle of seniority. Towards the end of the first quarter of the 13th century, a policy of unification was successfully carried out by Casimir's eldest son Leszek the White, prince of Cracow. However during the dukes' assembly in Gąsawa in Great Poland in 1227, he was treacherously assassinated and his death opened up a new period of struggle for Cracow, which lasted for more than ten years and in which Conrad of Mazovia, Leszek's younger brother, took part. Successes in economic policy and in the struggle for power were scored by the Duke of Silesia (Wrocław), Henry the Bearded, grandson of Ladislaus the Exile. By way of protectorate and succession he gained possession of a considerable part of Silesia and added southern Little Poland and the Cracow region to his realm.

By the end of his lifetime, he was the most remarkable representative of the reigning dynasty. Like Leszek the White, he tried to revive the kingdom, and attempted to secure the royal title for his son, Henry the Pious, who, after his father's death in 1238, assumed dominion over the Cracow region and Silesia. However, these plans were soon frustrated by the first Tartar invasion.

In the early decades of the 13th century a considerable part of Asia was united under the Mongol empire which, following the death of Genghis Khan, broke up into smaller states. The Mongols continued their conquests and, having seized Kiev and subjugated Ruthenia, in 1241 undertook an expedition against Catholic Europe. One Mongol army crossed the Carpathians and defeated the Hungarian armies on the river Sajó, while another ravaged Little Poland and Silesia. Henry the Pious and the flower of Polish chivalry were killed during the Battle of Legnica. The skilful, lightly armed Mongol horsemen easily routed the heavily armed slow-moving Polish knights. The

Mongols also used the invention of fireworks which scared the horses of their opponent. Threat loomed over Europe. The Mongols, difficult to beat, were conceived of as devils from hell — in Greek *Tartarus* — hence the popular name of Tartars.

Action was taken to unify the countries of Europe in the face of this common danger and diplomatic and reconnaissance missions were dispatched to Asia. They were often prepared in the duchies of southern Poland, which bordered on the Ruthenian lands.

In the winter of 1259—60, the second Mongol invasion, supported by Ruthenian armies, devastated southern Poland. The memory of the Tartar invasions of the 13th century lives on in Polish tradition.

In the mid-13th century, the greatest authority among the Piasts was enjoyed by Boleslaus the Chaste, duke of Cracow-Sandomierz, who married Princes Kinga of Hungary However, he did not undertake any campaigns aimed at unifying the Polish lands and several times was forced to take the field against rebellious barons. The canonization of Stanislaus, Bishop of Cracow, in 1253 was of considerable importance as it contributed to the consolidation of Cracow's position when unification tendencies intensified in the second half of the 13th century. Boleslaus' successor, Leszek the Black, was a powerful ruler who looked to the towns, especially Cracow, for support against the lords. Despite the lack of central authority in the 13th century, periods of danger brought solidarity among many of the dukes. The first quarter of the 13th century witnessed increasing difficulties caused by incursions of Prussians and Sudovians. Armed expeditions were mounted. Missionary work among the Prussians was also undertaken, but without marked success. One of the greatest of the district princes, Conrad of Mazovia, in 1226 invited to Poland for defence purposes the Order of the Teutonic Knights, which had been founded during the crusades.

In the 12th century, the crusades united the rulers and knights of western Europe and also stirred the mass of the people. Polish knights rarely took part in them, since Poland, situated on the periphery of Christian Europe, had as neighbours pagan peoples, including the Prussians. Soon the Teutonic Knights, who had settled in the Chełmno region as vassals of the Polish princes, began the systematic conquest of Prussia in which they were assisted by knights from other countries of western Europe. The conquest of Prussia was completed in 1283. However, instead of being a protective shield on Poland's borders, the Teutonic Knights set up their own state, emancipated themselves from the influence of the Polish princes and towards the end of the century became a serious threat to the fragmented native principalities.

If in the political arena the 13th century was marked by a decline of Polish influence, the transformations which had taken place in this period considerably strengthened the country's economy and contributed to the development of its culture which found expression above all in courtly and chivalrous mores.

Social and Economic Transformations

For Poland and her neighbours in east-central Europe, the 13th century was a period of intensive development. It gave rise to new forms of social life which were to be characteristic of the pre-industrial epoch. Rural and urban communes arose.

From the mid-12th century onwards, the ruler began to confer partial exemptions from taxation and judicial services, known as immunities. Initially, the chief beneficiaries were Church institutions. Later, from the 13th century on, they were extended to the gentry and wealthier knights. This was the beginning of the lord's jurisdiction over his serfs, known as patrimonial jurisdiction. District princes, bishops and abbots attempted to attract native and foreign settlers by granting them temporary exemption from dues which was meant to help them establish new farms. Foreigners appeared in Silesia in the 13th century, and later in Great Poland and western Little Poland, and included representatives of various nationalities, although Germans predominated. The Polish princes, like the rulers of Bohemia and Hungary, allowed them to use their own laws.

Soon foreign laws, imported by Walloons and especially Germans, mainly from Saxony, began to be applied in founding new villages. Thus the German law emerged as the law of large landed property. This law facilitated the formation of dependent communes. However a considerable number of villages continued to be settled under Polish law which — as was the case with German law — underwent evolution. In the 14th and 15th centuries, the differences between villages established under Polish law and those settled under German law tended to disappear.

A village established "under German law" was subject to the authority of a *sołtys* (bailiff), later known as a *wójt*, who was delegated to represent the commune's liege lord and who administered justice. The villagers settled under German law obtained tracts of land in perpetual and hereditary tenancy, with the landlord retaining supreme authority. In this way a system known as divided possession arose. More lenient rules were also applied in regard to royal vassals and the lesser knights of the prince or king. A feudal hierarchy emerged in which people were distinguished by their degree of dependence. In the 13th and 14th centuries intensive clearing of forests took place and land was better cultivated owing to the introduction of the wheeled plough with mould-board. Water mills — much more productive than querns or hand-mills — were built. New villages were allotted land in regular tracts divided into *łany* (from German *Lehen*, Polish *lenno* — fief) which constituted the basic unit for calculating the rent paid by villagers to the landlord. The system of three-crop rotation was introduced.

New town communes settled under German law in the 13th century generally arose in the vicinity of existing castle towns. The new towns replaced the former network of market centres in the vicinity of market towns. Rights and privileges granted to the towns facilitated the emergence of a new middle class. The towns, which were granted charters based on leasehold, had a regular pattern of streets around the market place. Booths selling meat and vegetables were erected around the market square. They were joined by drapers' shops in the second half of the 13th century, towards the end of which brick town halls were erected in the larger cities. At first weakly fortified, the cities soon acquired proper walls. Local self-government favoured closer links among the more powerful burghers and ensured the emergence of an urban culture which assumed greater importance in the 14th and 15th centuries. Urban development went hand in hand with the expansion of the money economy and the deepening division between urban and rural occupations. From the 12th century on, there was a growth in the internal significance of large-scale trade, which, via the routes leading from Silesia to the Pomeranian ports, especially Gdańsk, connected Poland with the developed economic centres of western Europe.

Despite the divisions of the 13th century, the feeling of unity among the Polish people was not lost. The concept of Polish nationhood — of the *gens polonica* — appears in the writings of native and foreign chroniclers. Poland as a political and geographic entity was strengthened by the organizational unity of the Church.

Soon the influx of Germans began to augment the feeling of solidarity not only among representatives of the lower, unprivileged strata, but also among the ruling circles. During the Council of Łęczyca in 1285, the Church decided that the heads of cathedral, monastery and parish schools should be people who knew Polish and could explain the works of learned writers to their pupils in this language. This is clear evidence of the development of education, which in the latter half of the 13th century assumed increasing importance.

The cultural heritage of the period of divisions, despite the weakening of the State, is considerable. In the second half of the 12th and in the 13th centuries, numerous Poles went abroad to study. One of them, Master Wincenty Kadłubek, Bishop of Cracow, was the author of an extensive *Polish Chronicle*. Church literature, which had links with the court and the new Dominican and Franciscan orders in urban centres, developed. The first preserved manuscripts of Polish religious poetry, including the beautiful *Bogurodzica* (Mother of God), a hymn not only sung in churches but by knights in battle, dates back to the 13th century. Liturgical music dates from the same period, one of the finest examples being *Christus surrexit*, from circa 1230. The manuscripts of these early compositions were discovered after the Second World War.

The chivalrous epic developed under western influence. The famous *Romance of Waltharius and Hiltgunt* was adapted to Polish conditions by introducing certain elements connecting the legend with Tyniec and Wiślica. Generally the theme of prepartition Poland predominated. For instance the famous voivode of the mid-12th century, Piotr Włostowic, became the hero of a Polish chivalrous legend in which the motifs of courage, loyalty and treachery combine with the motifs of penance and generosity, and church donations in human memory covered the whole of Poland.

Together with chivalrous literature the custom of knightly games came to Poland, especially tournaments, which were fought in the presence of the ladies of the court who crowned the victors.

The Kingdom United

Economic development and the expansion of towns and villages at the end of the 13th century strengthened economic ties between the districts, especially between Great Poland, Cracow and Silesia. The unification idea was supported by various social strata. It was taken up by Przemysł II, Duke of Great Poland, who in 1295 had himself crowned king of Poland in Gniezno. However, the growth in this ruler's importance disturbed the margraves of Brandenburg, who had him treacherously assassinated in Rogoźno in 1296. The king's death gave rise to a prolonged struggle for power in which the most supporters were initially won by King Wenceslas of Bohemia, the strongest pretender to the throne. In 1300, having captured Great Poland and Pomerania, Wenceslas had himself crowned King of Poland. His principal contender, the modest but exceptionally tenacious Duke of Kuyawy, Ladislaus the Short, had to flee the country.

The rule of the Bohemian Premyslids lasted six years. In 1306, after the death of Wenceslas III, Ladislaus the Short, with the support of the knights and part of the towns, entered Cracow, after previously occupying the Sandomierz and part of the Cracow regions.

Pomerania also recognized the rule of Ladislaus the Short. Soon, however, as a result of treachery by the noble Święca family, the Brandenburgians appeared in Pomerania. Called upon to help, the Teutonic Knights removed the Brandenburgians, but treacherously slaughtered the Polish garrison in Gdańsk and occupied this district in 1308—9.

Despite defeats and internal centrifugal tendencies (for example, the revolt of the larger towns in Little Poland and some monasteries commanded by Albert, *wójt* of Cracow), despite the constant threat represented by the Luxemburg dynasty in Bohemia, the Mark of Brandenburg in the west and the Teutonic Knights in the north, Ladislaus the Short united two important districts, Great and Little Poland.

As a result, he was able to conduct an active external policy and regain the Polish crown with the help of the Avignon curia. His coronation on 2 January 1320 in Cracow was the finishing touch in the country's unification, which was supported by the knights, a considerable proportion of the magnates and the clergy. Ladislaus the Short was not, however, strong enough to attempt the annexation of the Silesian duchies. Nor was he able to regain Pomerania, despite the fact that he won his suit before the papal legate against the Teutonic Knights (Inowrocław 1320—21). Later he allied himself with Lithuania, which was also threatened by the Teutonic Knights (1325). His reign saw the beginning of a period of bitter wars against the Order, of which the most famous episode was the Battle of Płowce (1331).

A marked growth in the importance of Poland and her neighbours, Bohemia and Hungary, is observable in the Europe of the 14th century. The rapid socio-economic and cultural development of this region occurred at a time when the countries of western and southern Europe were experiencing a serious crisis, aggravated by the effects of the Black Death which decimated the population of the best cultivated areas, and especially the larger towns. Destructive wars, the worst being the Hundred Years' War between England and France, also played nc little part. These changes lessened the gap between the new countries of central and eastern Europe and the most advanced countries of southern and western Europe, which had benefited to a greater extent from the heritage of ancient civilization.

In Poland, these changes were most noticeable during the reign of Casimir the Great, son of Ladislaus the Short. Casimir's reign brought a steady growth in Poland's importance in the international arena, observable both in the economic and political fields. Casimir continued his father's policies in trying to unite the country and expand the kingdom's boundaries. The basis of his policies was friendship and cooperation with Angevin Hungary and the Avignon curia. Thanks to his active and skilful diplomacy, he avoided, at the price of necessary concessions, war on two fronts with stronger opponents (the Kingdom of Bohemia and the Teutonic Knights). During the congress of Višegrad in 1339, he concluded an agreement with Charles Robert, King of Hungary, which stipulated that the Polish throne was to pass into Angevin hands should he, Casimir, die without a successor.

Despite the decree of the legate court favouring Poland, attempts to regain territories seized by the Teutonic Knights ended in an unfavourable compromise. The Bohemian king, John of Luxemburg, supported the interests of the Teutonic Knights. In 1343, during the Congress of Kalisz, Casimir signed a treaty with the latter under which he granted them Gdańsk Pomerania, Chełmno and Michałów, in return for Kuyawy and the Dobrzyń region. The signing of this treaty resulted in a long period of peace and gave the ruler a free hand in other political fields.

Under the terms of an earlier treaty, after the death of Boleslaus Trojdenowicz who governed Ruthenian Halicz and Vladimir (1340), Casimir became the ruler of these Ruthenian principalities. In the same year, he occupied Lvov and brought the Ruthenian lands under the Polish Crown on the basis of a personal union. He was less successful in regard to Silesia, which had absorbed his father, Ladislaus the Short, especially in the later years of his reign.

Casimir combined his political activities with attempts to promote the economic advancement of the country. He supported the development of leasehold settlement in the countryside and extended the protection of the Crown to the towns, especially in Little Poland. He was concerned about the development of international trade, which expanded considerably after the acquisition of Ruthenia. Turkish expansion limited the possibilities of trade with the East via the Mediterranean basin, and the land routes from Asia through southern Poland to the West thus gained in importance. Besides the merchants of Wrocław, those of Cracow and, to a lesser extent as yet, Lvov, actively participated in this trade.

The conclusion of peace with the Teutonic Knights resuscitated trade with the Prussian towns of Toruń and Gdańsk. To some degree, Poland's trade role during this period was that of an intermediary. Hungarian copper, for instance, which was sought in the West, was transported by way of Poland to the Baltic ports. On this transit route rivalry between the Prussian towns on the one hand and Cracow and other centres in Little Poland on the other, led to trade wars in which the burghers of Little Poland received active support from the king.

The king also directed his attention to administrative reforms, as well as to the administration of the crown lands, the efficient organization of which meant a considerable contribution to the royal treasury.

During the reign of Casimir the Great, Poland covered an area of nearly 270,000 sq. km. and there was a significant rise in the country's population, which is estimated to have numbered from two to two-and-a-half million inhabitants. The number and prosperity of the towns also grew considerably. In the larger urban centres there was an increase in specialization among craftsmen. The commodity-money economy expanded and the village population prospered. The towns of this period became polyglot centres whose population, apart from Poles, contained Germans, Jews, Italians, Bohemians and Hungarians. In Lvov Armenians acquired great importance. As a result of the incorporation of Ruthenia, the kingdom of Casimir the Great became a multinational state, similar to neighbouring Hungary, the state of the Teutonic Knights, and Lithuania.

Casimir the Great was an enlightened ruler, aware of his role in strengthening the foundations of the monarchy in Poland. While giving his support to the lower estates, especially the burghers and the lesser gentry, he ruled with an iron hand, to the annoyance of the magnates whose power was again on the increase.

Casimir attached great importance to legislation and had separate statutes drafted for Great Poland and Little Poland. The last of these, proclaimed at the Congress of Wiślica (the Wiślica Statutes), constitute the foundation of Polish written legislation, which in the 14th century took on permanent significance.

Finally, it is worth noting the king's patronage in the field of culture and art, especially architecture. It is said of Casimir that "he found Poland built in wood and left it built in brick". The funds of the royal treasury enabled him to build fortified castles and provide numerous towns with fortified walls, thus improving the country's defences. The king also paid a great deal of attention to military reforms.

Among the cultural initiatives undertaken by Casimir the Great during the last years of his rule, the founding of the Studium Generale in Cracow in 1364, was the most important, for it made Cracow the second city in central Europe — after Prague — to have a university. The king placed great emphasis on education; numerous schools were founded in his reign, the level of education rose, the number of libraries increased, and there was a growing tendency to make use of official documents.

The reign of Louis d'Anjou, King of Hungary, the successor to the Polish throne following the Angevin agreement, was in many respects the antithesis to that of Casimir. Louis, who was interested primarily in Hungary, rarely resided in Poland and as a result ruled through his governors general and through his mother, Elizabeth, daughter of Ladislaus the Short. In order to gain popularity and insure the succession to the throne for one of his daughters, Louis issued the Kosice Privilege in 1374 granting extensive privileges to the Polish magnates and knights, thus beginning the period of gentry privileges in Poland. He also renounced by this act taxes on the knights' estates with the exception of a tax of two groats per *łan* of serf-tilled land, and offered not to levy higher taxes without the consent of the gentry. The clergy soon received similar privileges.

Louis continued Casimir's policies in Ruthenia, maintained leasehold colonization and conferred endowments on the magnates and knights, mainly in Little Poland. In 1375, he formed a Roman Catholic archbishopric with its seat in Halicz, which was later transferred to Lvov, as well as a number of other sees (earlier Casimir the Great had seen to the restitution of the metropolis of the Eastern rite, subordinate to the patriarchate in Constantinople).

The Reign of the Jagiellons

During the rule of the Angevins in Poland, real power was exercised by a group of powerful nobles which gathered round the courts of Ladislaus the Short and Casimir the Great. They allowed no German prince, nor Duke Siemowit of Mazovia, to assume the Polish throne, and at the same time strove to gain the support of the Grand Duchy of Lithuania as a partner in the struggle with the Teutonic Order. The Lithuanian state at the time included the greater part of the western territories of Russia, which was weakened by Tartar pressure. On the northwestern frontier, however, Lithuania suffered losses as a result of pressure from the Teutonic Knights.

After Louis' death, the nobles prevented Sigismund of Luxemburg, husband of Louis' oldest daughter, Maria, from ascending the throne. They recognized the rights of her sister Jadwiga but forced her to break off her engagement with William of Austria. In 1385 in Krevo, they concluded a treaty with Jagiello, Grand Duke of Lithuania. Under the provisions of the treaty, Jagiello was converted and christened Ladislaus, pledged that Lithuania would be converted to the Latin rite, married Queen Jadwiga and became the new ruler of Poland. In this manner, the Polish Kingdom was joined with Lithuania on the basis of a personal union.

The union with Lithuania strengthened the Polish Kingdom. For Lithuania, the political alliance with Poland meant protection from the Teutonic Knights, for the conversion of pagan Lithuania removed the ideological justification for their expansion. Soon the aid which had long flowed from the West to the state of the Teutonic Knights, was reduced.

Poland was alive at this time to the possibilities of exerting cultural influence in the north-east. The eyes of Poles were opened to the significance of this fact chiefly by their antagonism to the Teutonic Knights. For this reason, the need for the renovation and expansion of the university founded by Casimir the Great was emphasized with increasing urgency in enlightened court circles in Cracow. Founded in 1400, the Cracow Academy soon became a strong centre of learning, closely connected with the court on the one hand, and the Cracow burghers on the other. In the years immediately following the surprisingly strong influence of this new university on the cultural development of Polish society can already be observed. The intensive development of education was a significant factor in the growth of a middle class culture, whose influence spread at this time to the knights and the nobility.

The outbreak of a conflict with the Teutonic Order was imminent since Jagiello's wise policies limited the intrigues of the Teutonic Knights in Lithuania. Since 1401, the Grand Duke of Lithuania was Witold, who acknowledged Jagiello's suzerainty. A plan for joint action on the part of the Polish and Lithuanian armies was worked out at the outbreak of the war with the Teutonic Order in 1409, and the combined armies defeated the Knights on 15 July 1410 at the Battle of Grunwald, one of the greatest battles of the Middle Ages. The Grand Master of the Order, Ulrich von Jungingen, and most of his knights were killed. Lithuania regained Samogitia. Yet as a result of the intervention of Sigismund of Luxemburg, who defended the Knights in the international arena, Jagiello was not able to take complete advantage of his great military victory, despite the fact that weakening of the Order opened the way to a favourable solution of the Gdańsk Pomerania problem. Nor did military and diplomatic struggle with the Teutonic Order cease.

In this period we observe a steady growth of Polish influence in international affairs, and Polish delegations actively participated in various councils. The victory of Grunwald resulted in the gain of the Pomeranian duchy of Słupsk. The Bohemian

Hussites at this time turned to Poland for help and were anxious for Ladislaus Jagiello, or another member of the Jagiellon dynasty, to accept the Bohemian crown. However, a number of magnates, headed by Zbigniew of Oleśnica, bishop of Cracow and later cardinal, were opposed to this plan. In 1420 Jagiello had to refuse the Bohemian crown and four years later in Wieluń he was forced to issue an anti-Hussite edict and to call back Polish troops from Bohemia.

During Jagiello's reign several privileges were granted to the magnates and knights, starting in 1388. The most important of these was a royal undertaking that no member of the nobility could be imprisoned without due process of law. By such acts the king intended to gain the support of representatives of the privileged estate for himself and his successors in Poland.

After Jagiello's death, Zbigniew of Oleśnica was the regent from 1434, in the name of the minor, Ladislaus III. As an important power, the Polish-Lithuanian state continued to participate in the politics of central Europe.

In 1438, after the death of Sigismund of Luxemburg, the Bohemian Utraquists offered to hand over Silesia, if Ladislaus Jagiello's younger son (Casimir) would accept the crown. However, the magnates, led by Bishop Zbigniew of Oleśnica, defeated the gentry's attempt at a pro-Hussite uprising in Poland and prevented Jagiello's son from accepting the Bohemian throne. In 1440, Casimir the Jagiellonian was called to the throne of the Grand Duchy of Lithuania, and Lithuania's union with Poland was thus severed. On the other hand, the sixteen-year-old Polish king, Ladislaus III, was enthroned as King of Hungary in 1440. In this manner, Poland found herself in an anti-Turkish coalition since the Turks, who at this time were extending their conquests in the Balkans, were threatening the Hungarian state. In 1444, the Hungarian armies were defeated in a battle with the Turks at Varna. The king and a great number of his knights were killed.

In 1447, Grand Duke Casimir of Lithuania, who inherited the Polish throne from his brother, re-established the Polish-Lithuanian union. In internal affairs, the king, who was opposed to the coalition of nobles headed by Zbigniew of Oleśnica, gained the support of the knights. Later, he turned his attention to the towns, to which he attempted to extend his protection. He effectively opposed papal fiscal polices by skilfully appointing his candidates to bishoprics. He also incorporated the Silesian duchies of Oświęcim and Zator. In the middle of the 15th century, there was a sharpening of conflicts between the rich and powerful Prussian towns and the Teutonic Knights. Also among the knights of Prussian Pomerania the rule of the Teutonic Knights was becoming less popular. A confederation of nobles and Prussian towns was formed, and the larger cities repudiated the authority of the Teutonic Order and declared their allegiance to the Polish king. This resulted in the outbreak of what came to be known as the Thirteen Years' War (1454—66). Initially it seemed as if the king, who was allied with the patriciate of the Prussian towns, would gain an easy victory over the Order. But the opening phase of the struggle revealed the unsuitability of an army based on the levée en masse, even if it had won the day at Grunwald, less than half a century earlier. Growing prosperity had changed the knights from warriors into landowners whose chief concern was husbandry rather than battle. What was more, the knights, assembled in their camp near Nieszawa (1454), demanded privileges from the king for the price of their participation in the war. Among other things, the king had to pledge that in future he would not take important decisions without the consent of the gentry. In this manner, the Nieszawa Privileges became the factual basis of Polish parliamentarism. The significance of the gentry diets (*sejmiki*) and general diets (seyms) increased. Deputies were elected at land diets representing the gentry and the chapters. They constituted the Chamber of Deputies in the emerging Parliament, while the Royal Council began to evolve into a second chamber called the Senate.

During the Thirteen Years' War, the bulk of the fighting was undertaken by mercenary regiments engaged by the Prussian towns and the king. Victory was finally achieved, and under the terms of the peace treaty signed in Toruń in 1466, the Teutonic Knights relinquished their hold on the Chełmno region, Gdańsk Pomerania and Żuławy. Warmia, which had been ruled by local bishops, also became part of the Kingdom as a fief of the Polish monarch. The regained territory constituted a separate Prussian province whose estates had the right to separate representation. From then on, it was known as Royal Prussia, to distinguish it from the remaining Teutonic state. The Grand Master moved from Malbork to Königsberg and pledged allegiance to the Polish king. The most prosperous towns, especially Gdańsk, retained their privileged position.

The peace of Toruń opened wider opportunities for trade with the Prussian towns, especially Gdańsk and Elbląg. As early as the first half of the 15th century, the Vistula became an important trade route. The rise in the demand for grain in the populated regions of north-western Europe (Flanders, the Low Countries, England) resulted in greater grain exports. Manorial farms were largely transformed into commercial enterprises producing grain for sale and thus requiring more manpower. Both the magnates and the gentry tried to secure this by imposing additional labour duties on their peasants, thus turning them into serfs.

The conclusion of the Peace of Toruń enabled Casimir the Jagiellonian to engage in an active dynastic policy. During the war in 1462, he signed an alliance in Głogów with the Bohemian king, George of Podiebrad, whereby, after George's death (1471), Casimir's son Ladislaus was to succeed to the Bohemian throne. In 1490, Ladislaus the Jagiellon succeeded to the Hungarian throne as well. The influence of the Jagiellonian dynasty in Europe was at its peak. Four countries, Poland, Lithuania, Bohemia and Hungary — in effect all of central and eastern Europe — found themselves under Jagiellonian rule. Only the small duchy of Muscovy, which had begun the arduous task of uniting the Russian territories, remained beyond the reach of Jagiellonian rule in the East. The Jagiellonian dynasty became one of the most influential ruling families in Europe, and their territory exceeded that of all contemporary ruling houses, not excluding the Habsburgs.

Society and Culture in the Late Middle Ages

Towards the end of the Middle Ages, society was divided into estates, of which that of the knights and gentry held the most privileged position. As in Hungary, the Polish gentry was numerous and internally differentiated. In some parts of Poland, especially in the Łuków region in Mazovia and in Great and Little Poland in the vicinity of former ducal castles, there were knights who owned small manorial farms. The burghers constituted a separate estate, but, unlike the gentry, they did not have general privileges as an estate. Their situation differed depending on whether they lived in royal towns or small, particularly private, towns.

The peasant estate was without any public rights or privileges. However, owing to the period of economic prosperity, they were becoming richer and were establishing closer links with towns which constituted the main market for agricultural produce. This in turn gave the peasants access to the products of urban craftsmen.

Many peasants moved to the small towns which were developing in this period. So did representatives of the gentry, who sought opportunities for improving their lot. At the same time the prospering burghers, especially those of Cracow and Lvov, established marriage relationships with the richer gentry and nobles. They bought landed estates and some of the wealthier families moved to the countryside and obtained gentry privileges.

A characteristic feature of the structure of the late medieval estate of gentry and knights was the considerable significance of clan relationships, especially of a heraldic character, based on the principle of kinship, often fictitious, which found expression in the coat-of-arms, slogan and clan name. In the 12th and 13th centuries, clans were formed among nobles where blood ties and good descent were particularly valued. With the division of society into estates, the clans also embraced middle and lower knights. There began to emerge clans of lesser knights which adopted the arms of the lands they inhabited, with which arms emblazoned on their banners they went into battle. Many such clans were formed by small groups of warrior knights settled in a given region, such as Średniawici and Drużynici on the Śreniawa river in the Cracow area.

Internal relations in the 15th century were characterized by the growing influence of the nobles, whose rivalry with the gentry was significant for the state's socio-political structure. The kings, threatened by the growing influence of the nobles, especially those in Little Poland, tried to prevent them from forming a separate estate, as they had done in Bohemia and Hungary. In this the monarchy was successful. The nobles remained formally a part of the gentry estate, but the royal council, which was later transformed into the higher chamber (Senate) of the Polish parliament, was composed nearly exclusively of them. On the other hand, the land diet, which in the late 15th century evolved into the Seym, was also made up of nobles, especially, but not exclusively, of those who held land offices.

In the development of medieval learning and culture in Poland a particularly important role was played by burghers and people of plebeian origin, as opportunities for intellectual creativity were not restricted to the privileged estate. Throughout this period it was the domain of the clergy and those connected with it. On the other hand artistic creativity was of a handicraft character and considered an unworthy occupation for representatives of the privileged estate.

The earliest Polish scholars are encountered in the 13th century, working mainly in foreign countries. Only after the founding of the Cracow University did scholarship start to develop in Poland itself.

In the 13th century Cracow scholars took an active part in European learning, and in such disciplines as international law, philosophy and astronomy, presented innovatory ideas. Stanisław of Skarbimierz (?—1431) defended the view that natural law is the same for everybody. Together with Paweł Włodkowic, (c. 1370—c. 1435) he wrote on the admissibility of wars in international relations and opposed the practice of converting pagans by the sword. In the second half of the 15th century, Jan Ostroróg (1436—1501), a representative of a well-known noble family, formulated a programme of state reform. Like thinkers of the early 15th century, he propounded the idea of state sovereignty and independence from the Empire. Thus current problems of international and internal policy found expression in theoretical thought, which testifies to the fact that Poland in the late Middle Ages had ceased to be a peripheral country and had become one proclaiming the ideas of humanism.

Even before the 13th century, the penalty of being sold into slavery, which initially encompassed the entire family of the accused, was abolished. The lagislation of the 13th century contains traces of the humanitarian idea of extending protection to the poor; such traces are to be found in a list of the provisions of Polish common law prohibiting confiscation of the bundle of a pauper. Responsibility for executing these provisions fell to church institutions and towns, since it was the towns in which loose and sick people sought asylum. The system of corporal punishments was restricted, with such penalties as blinding or pulling out the tongue being in practice abandoned. In general, however, there prevailed social inequality and the conflicts arising therefrom, which found expression in riots by town plebs against government by the patricians and peasant revolts caused by exploitation.

A characteristic feature of the late Middle Ages was considerable personal mobility. Polish knights went abroad to offer their services to foreign lords, some going as far afield as North Africa. Craftsmen travelled from town to town in search of bread and apprentices in search of masters. Lay and church politicians carried on large-scale diplomatic campaigns. Peasants crossed the Polish border to settle in the forests of Prussia. Migration started to the less populated regions of Lithuania and Ruthenia.

In the late Middle Ages an important role was played by the Gothic style, similar to the Gothic in other countries. It was first introduced in towns and courts, and in the 15th century rural stone churches, burghers' houses and country manors were built in this style. Country residences were usually fortified, the only stone element being a defence tower. Wooden houses were also built, especially wooden churches with Gothic elements, chiefly ogival windows and portals.

In large towns, the number of masons, carpenters, as well as painters, miniature makers and sculptors, increased. The most important town was Cracow whose influence spread to the whole of Little Poland and the neighbouring part of Hungary (present-day northern Slovakia). The most prominent artist was Wit Stwosz of Nuremberg who lived in Cracow in the second half of the 15th century. His most important work was done in Poland, above all the grand altar piece in St. Mary's Church in Cracow.

Sculpture, chiefly in wood, developed in two directions: secular and mystical. The former was characterized by the masterful rendition of the beauty of human figure, especially the face and hands, while the latter employed deformation in order to express ecstasy and suffering; this deformation, subordinated to the rigours of the late Gothic, later developed into mannerist art which was to produce many outstanding works.

The world of medieval Poland was a colourful world, a world of the deep hues of church interiors, of richly decorated portals. It was to be found in royal residences and wealthy burgher houses where wall paintings merged with colourful tapestries illuminated by the light of candles in candelabra and sometimes — as in the vast Gothic churches — in chandeliers. For throughout the Middle Ages great importance was attached to light and during the Gothic period special effects based on the play of colours were achieved by painting the panes of large

windows and imaginative placing of candles. Colour and
richness of dress, being evidence of the wealth and social position, were also prized. Hence attempts to place restrictions on
the dress of burghers and the vestments of the clergy, who according to the principles of the Christian religion were supposed to wear simple clothes and appear in full splendour only
for religious rites.

After Casimir the Great had subjugated part of Ruthenia, Poland also came into contact with Oriental culture, both through
trade with the Armenians living in Lvov and through the wars
in the East. These contacts dated from the late Middle Ages and
were manifested above all in dress. The conquest of Ruthenia
and the union with Lithuania brought Byzantine influences,
while Balkan influences came from Hungary, Moldavia and Wa-
lachia. In the 15th century, thanks chiefly to the patronage of
Ladislaus Jagiello, frescoes painted in the Byzantine-Slavo-
nic convention appeared in some of the more important churches, including Gniezno and Wawel Cathedrals, Holy Cross
Abbey and Sandomierz collegiate church. Thus the late Middle
Ages provided creative impulses for the arts and learning to an
extent not fully realized yet, and exerted a considerable influence on the further development of civilization in Poland.

Tadeusz Lalik

Poland's Golden Age under the Last Jagiellons

After the death of Casimir the Jagiellonian, the Polish-Lithuanian union was temporarily severed; the younger of the great
king's sons, Alexander, received the Lithuanian throne while
the elder, John Albert, was elected King of Poland. John Albert,
intelligent and ambitious, drew his support from the middle
gentry, thus continuing his father's policies. The opening of
his reign saw the final shaping of the Polish Seym. From this
moment until the partitions brought the first Commonwealth
(Polish *rzeczpospolita*: etymologically identical with Latin *res
publica*) to an end, the General Assembly consisted of two
chambers: the Senate, formerly the Privy Council, and the
Chamber of Deputies composed of delegates chosen at the land
diets.

In 1497, the king undertook a military expedition in order to
recover from the Turks the Black Sea ports of Akkerman and

Kilia, and strengthen the feudal dependence of Moldavia. However, the expedition failed as Moldavia sided with Turkey against Poland and the retreating Polish levies suffered a defeat in the Bukovina, of which it was said later that "under King Albert the gentry perished".

After John Albert's death, Alexander was installed on the Polish throne and the personal union with the Grand Duchy of Lithuania was re-established. Already towards the end of the reign of Casimir the Jagiellonian the eastern boundaries of Lithuania, about 95 miles from Moscow, began to shrink. At this time, Ivan III, Grand Duke of Muscovy, began to unite the Russian lands, a project which included extending the boundaries of his dominions to the Ruthenian territories of the Jagiellonian state.

While Alexander was in Lithuania, the work of government was carried on by the senators who belonged to old magnate families. This roused the gentry opposition, led by Chancellor Jan Łaski, to act. In 1504 the Seym passed resolutions directed against the magnates, which forbade the holding of several high offices by one person and limited the distribution of royal lands. The foundations of government in the Commonwealth of the gentry were established a year later. In a decree issued at the Seym of Radom, the king pledged himself neither to levy taxes nor pass new laws without the consent of the Senate and the Chamber of Deputies: *Nihil novi... sine communi consensu* (nothing new... without common consent).

With interruptions the war with Muscovy lasted until 1537, that is also during the reign of Casimir the Jagiellonian's youngest son, Sigismund I the Old. The most important events came in 1514: one was the loss of Smolensk, a large city and important strategic stronghold, while the other was brilliant victory at Orsza of the Polish-Lithuanian armies under Konstanty Ostrogski.

In 1515, a high price had to be paid for the break-up of the dangerous alliance between the Emporor Maximilian I and the ruler of Muscovy when, at the Congress of Vienna, King Sigismund approved his brother's concessions in favour of the Habsburgs as regards the latter's dynastic rights to the Bohemian and Hungarian crowns. When Louis, son of Ladislaus Jagiellon, was killed in 1526 in battle with the Turks at Mohács, the Habsburgs gained Bohemia and Hungary.

Thus ended the 36 year rule of the Jagiellons in four states.

Unfortunately each of these states represented different interests (for example while Hungary was in favour of a war against Turkey, Poland was against it) and therefore they failed to form a uniform political entity.

The Grand Masters of the Order of the Teutonic Knights had not paid homage to the Polish king since John Albert's time. However, when Albert of Hohenzollern (nephew of Sigismund I), sought to sever the fealty owed the Crown, and allied himself with Muscovy, Poland struck at Teutonic Prussia. The war, which lasted from 1519 to 1521, ended in a victory for Poland, although the final solution was a compromise by which German Prussia was merely transformed into a secular duchy (the Order of the Teutonic Knights was secularized and adopted the new Lutheran faith). Albert, the Grand Master, became a hereditary duke, owing fealty to the Polish king and, at the expiration of his dynasty, the Duchy of Prussia was to be joined to Poland. This treaty, signed in 1525 in Cracow, separated the Prussian State from the Pope and Emperor and ensured considerable Polish influence. Only the later concessions made by a weakened Commonwealth showed the disastrous consequences of such an arrangement.

At the beginning of the 16th century Boguslaus X, Duke of Western Pomerania, strove to obtain political support from Poland, but that chance was not taken for fear of worsening relations with the Empire and Brandenburg. An undoubted success of the policies of Sigismund I was the incorporation of Mazovia after the Mazovian Piast dynasty came to an end in 1526.

The privileges granted the gentry by previous kings, especially the *Nihil Novi* law, ensured them full political rights and exclusive influence on the Seym, which in future was to be the chief organ of state power. The gentry in Poland were quite numerous (about 10 per cent of the population), although a considerable proportion were lesser gentry, who did not own serfs and cultivated their own land. The economic base of the middle gentry and magnates were estates worked by serfs. In the 16th century, the number and size of such manor farms increased, and there was a corresponding rise in the export of grain abroad, via Gdańsk, by sea to the countries of western Europe. The gentry, exploiting their own political predominance in accordance with the interests of their estate, aspired to gain privileges which would limit the rights of the peasants and burghers. John Albert's privilege of 1496 tied the peasants to the land, i.e. their right to leave their village to learn a trade or attend school in the towns was considerably curtailed. In the first quarter of the 16th century, when the king waived his right to judge disputes between the gentry and the peasants, the peasants became completely subjugated to the rule of their masters and serfdom was further consolidated. The gentry limited the rights of the burghers by preventing them from purchasing land or holding high Church offices. It imposed maximum prices in municipal trade while gentry trade was duty-free. Despite this, the economic situation of the peasants and the burghers under the last Jagiellons was reasonably good while the larger cities, as centres of international trade, became more prosperous.

During the reign of Sigismund I, the middle gentry came out against the magnates, and also against the policy of the royal court. The circumspect and thrifty monarch's energies declined as the years went by, which meant that his second wife, the Italian princes Bona Sforza, exerted a stronger influence on the government (from 1518 onwards). She sought to strengthen the dynasty's position by redeeming mortgaged royal lands and also attempted to create a court party of magnates dependent on her favours.

A programme of state reform under the slogan of "execution of the law and execution of the estates" put forward as a result of the maturing political opposition of the gentry, called for the modernization of existing policies together with the restoration of former just rights, which had not been executed previously, and the return of illegally distributed royal lands. Besides this, the internally divided "execution" movement, as it was known, also introduced many other demands. These demands revealed, among other things, the gentry's attitude to the Habsburgs who, while having many supporters among the Polish magnates, as advocates of absolute rule were regarded by the squires as enemies of gentry democracy.

In Lvov, in 1537, the "execution" movement led to a rebellion of the mass levies called up for an expedition against Moldavia. As a result, Sigismund the Old, together with the Senate, was forced to make concessions to the gentry. This first Polish rebellion was contemptuously dubbed the "War of the Hens" by the magnates, from the great number of hens eaten by the rebels.

Sigismund I's only son, Sigismund Augustus, for many years based his government, like his father, on cooperation with the Senate. The beginning of his reign was marked by a struggle for the recognition of his marriage with Barbara Radziwiłł, whom he married secretly in 1547. The gentry and crown magnates, who supported Bona's hostile attitude to Barbara, were strongly opposed to the king's union with the Radziwiłłs, a powerful Lithuanian family. Through his clever tactics, Sigismund Augustus was nevertheless able to secure Barbara's coronation (1550).

In 1562, the monarch gave his support to the Chamber of Deputies, which was controlled by the "execution" party headed by such outstanding leaders as Mikołaj Sienicki, Hieronim Ossoliński and Rafał Leszczyński. The reform movement now brought results in the shape of the re-seizure of royal lands, which added to the resources of the royal treasury, and the setting up of a standing army for the protection of Poland's southeastern borders (for whose upkeep one quarter of the revenue from the royal lands was set aside). A closer unification of the crown lands with Royal Prussia was carried out and a real union with Lithuania was concluded.

These were years of onerous conflict over Livonia, in which Polish-Lithuanian interests conflicted with those of Muscovy. For centuries Livonia had been dominated by a local branch of the Order of the Teutonic Knights. When the eastern borders of this region were invaded by the armies of Ivan the Terrible, and in the north the Swedes seized Estonia, Gotthard von Kettler, the Grand Master, secularized the Order and recognized the overlordship of the Polish king. As a result, Livonia was joined to Lithuania and Poland, and Kettler became Duke of Courland, owing fealty to the Commonwealth. The war over Livonia, which, apart from the Jagiellon state and Muscovy, involved also Sweden and Denmark, became the first northern war over control of the Baltic area (1563—70). In the course of the struggle Sigismund Augustus organized a standing navy, for which purpose a Naval Commission was created in 1568, whose work was, however, interrupted by the king's death.

Polish efforts to establish a closer union with the Grand Duchy of Lithuania had the approval of the Lithuanian gentry, which was just emerging as a separate estate and anxious to gain equal rights with the Polish gentry. The powerful Lithuanian magnates, on the other hand, were opposed to this union. Difficult and protracted negotiations were finally concluded during the Polish-Lithuanian Seym in Lublin in 1569. A few years earlier, Sigismund Augustus, who lacked a successor, had renounced his hereditary rights to the Lithuanian throne. At the Lublin Seym he broke the resistance of the Lithuanian magnates and detached Podlasie, Volhynia, Podolia and the region of Kiev from the Grand Duchy, incorporating them into Poland. By the act of 1 July 1569, Lithuania and Poland were united as the Commonwealth of the Two Nations, having not only a single monarch, but also a common Seym. On the other hand, government offices, the treasury and armed forces remained separate.

The Union of Lublin, a consequence of the evolution of Polish-Lithuanian relations since Jagiello's reign, was one of the most momentous events in the history of eastern Central Europe. It accelerated the economic, social and cultural development of the Grand Duchy of Lithuania, and resulted in the polonization of the Lithuanian and Ruthenian gentry, who obtained the same rights as the Polish gentry; thus Polish cultural influence spread as far as the Russian state. On the other hand, this process of polonization and the expansion of the Polish gentry to the eastern territories was bound to lead to a rise in national antagonisms. The Union also contributed to the weakening of the balance within the gentry and the concentration of power in the hands of the magnates.

The year 1569 marked the end of the process of the Commonwealth's formation as a multinational state, similar in this respect to the Habsburg monarchy and to certain other states at that time. Under the last Jagiellons, when Poland gradually began to get involved in the affairs of Lithuania and the latter's conflicts with Muscovy, she had to limit her political activity in the South and West. This meant a decline of interest in the ethnically Polish territories in the West.

The period of the last Jagiellons represened the greatest efflorescence in the history of old Poland. The country was large and affluent, experienced rapid economic progress and an increase in prosperity during a time of relative peace. The Polish Commonwealth occupied a strong position in the international arena. When many other states were developing the system of absolutism, in Poland a system of gentry democracy was in process of formation. The ruling class began to identify itself with the nation, and the concept of "Commonwealth" meant in fact a commonwealth of the gentry with the form of a monarchy.

The gentry's existing privileges, of which the most significant were personal immunity and the inviolability of property, were extended during this period to include freedom of faith.

By the twenties of the 16th century, the Reformation had reached the towns of Royal Prussia and part of Great Poland, giving rise to social radicalism, which manifested itself in serious plebeian revolts in Toruń, Gdańsk and Elbląg. Sigismund the Old sharply attacked the spread of dissent and social rebellion, although his son was more tolerant in religious matters. During the reign of Sigismund Augustus the Reformation made rapid headway, but was soon to suffer a setback.

While Lutheranism was supported by the urban middle class, Calvinism spread mostly among the gentry. In the mid-16th century, the Bohemian Brethren, continuators of the Hussite movement, settled in Great Poland, and in 1562—65 the Polish Brethren (Arians), who believed in the most radical theological (Antitrinitarianism) and social doctrines (they were against peasant serf labour), broke away from Calvinism. The idea of separation from Rome and the formation of a National Church was also mooted.

The Reformation, which aimed at the abolition of the landed property privileges of the clergy and their ecclesiastical juris-diction over the gentry, was largely a socio-political conflict with the Catholic clergy, especially the Church hierarchy. The dissenters vented these aims in the "execution" movement, which resulted in a law passed by the Seym forbidding the royal governors to implement verdicts passed by ecclesiastical courts (1563). The implementation of these demands led to a reduction of interest on the part of the mass of the gentry in the Reformation and marked the beginning of its decline. In 1570, Calvinists, Lutherans and Bohemian Brethren concluded the "Union of Sandomierz", in order jointly to defend themselves against the growing strength of the Catholic Counter-Reformation, the latter having been strengthened by the Jesuits brought to Poland in 1564.

After the death of Sigismund Augustus in 1573, under the terms of the Confederation of Warsaw, the gentry gained legal guarantees of religious freedom and equal rights for dissenters and Catholics. In practice other estates, with the exception of a few towns and some landed estates, also enjoyed these rights. The Polish peasantry remained true to Catholicism almost to a man. Religious tolerance can stand as a great achievement of Polish political thought and practice. For many of the countries then racked by religious wars, the Commonwealth represented a nation of religious asylum, where adherence to different creeds did not lead to the stake.

The 16th century is known as Poland's Golden Age in view of the cultural achievements to which favourable economic conditions, internal peace and the influence of Renaissance humanism and the Reformation, all contributed. The vernacular permeated all areas of social and cultural life and overcame the domination of Latin in writing, becoming increasingly refined as an instrument of communication in the process. The main reason was the need for disseminating new humanist ideals, above all those of the Reformation. And it was the Reformation that introduced the vernacular into religious rites and writings and forced the Catholic Church to go along with the process, albeit on a limited scale. Following the introduction of printing, which revolutionized the communication of ideas, written works achieved a larger circulation. In Poland the first printed works appeared in 1473 and the early 16th century saw a rapid development of printing, particularly in Cracow. This contributed to a uniformity of the Polish language, that is to the emergence of a national literary language.

There existed a fairly dense network of elementary parish schools, supplemented by new, secondary schools, mainly Protestant and later Jesuit. The Lutheran secondary schools in Gdańsk and Toruń almost evolved into academic institutions. On the other hand Cracow University, following a period of rapid development, turned back to old medieval ideals. Sons of the gentry and the burghers travelled to foreign universities, mainly in Italy and Germany

In the 16th century, Poland could vie with the rest of Europe in education and the arts, and made its own valuable contribution to world culture. The work of Nicolaus Copernicus (*De Revolutionibus Orbium Coelestium*) became a turning point in astronomy and had important philosophical consequences. Andrzej Frycz Modrzewski, advocate of the equlity of the estates before the law, postulated in his treatise *Commentariorum de Re-publica emendada* (1551—54), advanced ideas about government and law; this work was translated into Polish, German, Spanish. French and Russian (although the last two translations did not appear in print). The lyrics of Jan Kochanowski, the creator of modern Polish poetry, may be counted among masterpieces of European literature. The outstanding Renaissance composer Mikołaj Gomółka set to music Kochanowski's Polish translation of the Psalms of David.

Italian models in Renaissance architecture and sculpture were assimilated and adapted to Polish conditions. The first masterpieces of Renaissance architecture were the converted Wawel Castle with its cloistered courtyard and a chapel at Wawel Cathedral, both built at the instigation of King Sigismund the Old. These were followed by magnate residences and townhalls. Sculpture flourished in the form of sumptuous sarcophagi placed in churches and chapels by temporal and spiritual lords, the gentry and burghers. They included work by Italian artists and Jan Michałowicz of Urzędów, the most famous Polish sculptor.

Artistic crafts were the preserve of burghers and a few members of the peasantry. However in general the Polish Renaissance was due mainly to the gentry as the utilitarian humanist ideas appealed to this estate most of all. The medieval ideals of the knight and saint were replaced with the ideals of the landowner and citizen, who, while ready to fight when necessary, preferred a quiet, prosperous existence on his country estate.

The age of the Renaissance and Reformation also witnessed considerable progress in the development of Polish national awareness which meant something more than the awareness of affiliation to a state that encompassed various nations within a Commonwealth. National consciousness was promoted by the growing importance of the Polish language and its uniformity, the increasing political role of the gentry, the political and legal unification of the state, and the stronger economic and cultural links between the country's individual regions. All this served to forge closer ties between all the inhabitants of Poland who spoke Polish. However the 16th century was only the beginning of this process since it encompassed only the gentry, a part, perhaps the majority, of the burghers and a small proportion of the peasantry. It was in the 16th century too that the German burghers in the Commonwealth, with the exception of Royal Prussia, finally embraced the Polish language as their own.

During this period there emerged an idea which in the following

centuries was to hamper the growth of Polish national consciousness, according to which the concept of the nation was identified with the gentry only, irrespective of their ethnic identity,
and did not encompass the burghers and peasants. In his historical and geographical description of the Slavonic lands
(*Tractatus de duabus Sarmatiis, Asiana et Europiana*, 1517) Maciej
of Miechów made references to this view and derived the origins of the Poles from ancient Sarmatians. This myth was later
continued and developed by other writers and Sarmatia became synonymous with Poland and a Sarmatian with a Pole,
and, in effect, a Polish nobleman.

From "Gentry Democracy" to the Oligarchy of the Magnates

During the lifetime of Sigismund Augustus no arrangements had
been made for the functioning of the state in the absence of a
king, nor had any principles been worked out for the election
of a new king, all of which became necessary after the death of
the last Jagiellon. The head of state during the interregnum
was the Primate, who was known as the *interrex*. In 1573, the
Convocation Seym (so called as it was convoked to prepare for
the election) accepted the principle that the entire gentry had the
right to participate directly in the choosing of the king, that is
the principle of an election *viritim*. Against the background of
the times, this was a demagogic principle which only appeared
to strengthen the camp of the middle gentry, while in fact favouring the intrigues of the magnates and foreign states.
In the same year, the electoral seym formulated the most important principles underlying the political system of the Commonwealth, and these were soon after placed before the newly
elected king, Henry of Valois. Hereafter, every king-elect had
to pledge an oath of allegiance to the Henrician Articles, along
with additional individual obligations (known as *pacta conven-
ta*). The Henrician Articles guaranteed a free election, the convocation of the Seym at least every two years and the maintenance of a permanent advisory council of resident senators.
In the event of the king failing to keep to these obligations, the
Henrician Articles released the gentry from their oath of obe-
dience. This not only further limited the king's authority, but al-

so represented an attempt to control the monarchy and a threat of legal rebellion.

The French Crown Prince, Henry of Valois, who ruled Poland only a few months, secretly fled Cracow in order to assume the French throne when notified of the death of his brother, Charles IX.

At the next election a majority of the Senate proclaimed the Emperor Maximilian II king, while the gentry recognized Stephen Báthory, Duke of Transylvania, designating Anne the Jagiellonian, sister of Sigismund Augustus, as his bride. Báthory prevailed over the Habsburg and forced the Emperor's magnate supporters to submission, the resistance of Gdańsk having to be broken partly by concessions and partly by military force (1577). Báthory concentrated mainly on foreign policy and military matters, leaving internal affairs to be dealt with by his chancellor, Hetman Jan Zamoyski. Concerned about royal prerogatives, he did not always prove a skilful politician and often came in conflict with the gentry and the magnate opposition.

In order to gain the gentry's approval for high military taxes Stephen Báthory gave way to the earlier demands of the "execution" movement by establishing in 1578 a supreme court of the gentry — the Crown Tribunal. The Tribunal sat in Lublin and in Piotrków. Three years later, a Lithuanian Tribunal was set up (in Vilna, Novogrodek and Minsk). These tribunals, elected during annual diets, replaced the king's jurisdiction over the gentry.

Ivan the Terrible's invasion of Livonia in 1577 marked the outbreak of war.

The Polish army was reinforced by infantry regiments formed by Báthory from peasants on the royal estates. This talented military leader led three victorious compaigns against Muscovy in three consecutive years (1579—81), and conquered Polotsk, Velikiye Luki and laid siege to Pskov. The war, which was concluded by a truce signed in 1582 in Yam Zapolsky, strengthened the authority of the Commonwealth in Livonia and extended Lithuania's borders into the region of Polotsk. The king considered an invasion of Turkey, after first subjugating Russia, but his unexpected death put an end to these plans. In the third election, two candidates again emerged for the Polish crown — Sigismund Vasa, son of the Swedish King John III and Catherine the Jagiellonian, and the Habsburg Archduke Maximilian. Zamoyski's victory over Maximilian in the battle of Byczyna (1588) was the deciding factor in favour of Sigismund, a Jagiellon on the distaff side.

He was not liked by many of the gentry for his lack of skill in politics, his alignment with the Habsburgs and the influence the Jesuits had upon him.

In the years 1595—96, during the synods held in Brest Litovsk, the Orthodox Church in Poland accepted union with the Roman Church, subordinating itself to the Papacy. The Union of Brest was intended to make for the closer integration of the ethnically Ruthenian lands with Poland. Relations among national groups on these lands to a great extent reflected social relations, since the Ruthenian magnates and gentry became polonized and the Polish settlers in the Ukraine readily underwent assimilation (although some of them, impoverished gentry and, in part, the population of the towns preserved their separate identity). It was different only in Red Ruthenia, where the polonization of the towns, minor gentry and sometimes of the peasants as well, was more pronounced. Nationality and religion went hand in hand.

The plans associated with the Union of Brest failed, because most of the Ruthenian population rejected this union and attempts to impose it by force sharpened hostilities, especially since the supporters of Orthodoxy included the Cossacks. These were bodies of free peasants organized along military lines and consisting largely of fugitive serfs who had found sanctuary in the vastness of the Ukraine.

The hereditary Swedish throne was more important to Sigismund III than the elective Polish throne, which did not guarantee the interests of his dynasty. After his father's death in 1592, Sigismund Vasa became King of Sweden, but territorial conflicts over Estonia and opposition in Sweden to a joint king led to this dethronement. In response, the king granted northern Estonia to Poland, which led to a Swedish invasion of Livonia.

This was the beginning of a war which lasted, with intervals, from 1600 to 1629. The Poles, led by Jan Karol Chodkiewicz, compensated for the setbacks of the first period by a resounding victory in 1605 at Kirkholm.

The growing opposition of the gentry and a section of the magnates towards the policy of Sigismund III and his supporters, broke out in an uprising which, from the name of one of its leaders, was known as the Zebrzydowski Rebellion (1606—08). Despite the defeat of the rebels at Guzów (1607), the court faction had to give up all plans for strengthening royal authority. The rebellion undermined the monarch's power and brought no gains to the middle gentry, but it did enhance the position of the magnates. The rebels charged the king with supporting the False Dmitri's invasion of Muscovy. Some Polish magnates had indeed supplied this alleged son of Ivan the Terrible with military aid (1604—06). A few years later, the Commonwealth officially involved itself in a civil war for the throne of Muscovy. When Tsar Vasili Shuiski concluded an alliance with Sweden in 1609, Polish armies besieged Smolensk, which was gained only after two years of fighting. In the meantime, in 1610, Hetman Stanisław Żółkiewski crushed the main Russian army at Klushin and occupied Moscow, where Shuiski had already been dethroned. The son of Sigismund III, Ladislaus, was chosen as Tsar, but when the enemy consolidated his forces, in 1612 the Polish garrison in the Kremlin had to capitulate. Ladislaus' unsuccessful attempt to seize the crown of Muscovy ended in a truce at Deulino in 1619, by which the Commonwealth gained the territories of Smolensk, Chernigov and Novogrod Sieviezh.

Fearing a Swedish-Brandenburg alliance, Sigismund III resolved to conclude an agreement with the Elector of Brandenburg, to whom Ducal Prussia had passed after the local Hohenzollern line had died out. Henceforth, the links of fealty between the Duchy of Prussia and the Commonwealth began to weaken.

Cossack incursions into Turkish dominions, interventions by Polish magnates in Moldavia, the military aid granted to Turkey's enemies, the Habsburgs, and the Tartar invasions of Poland, all led to the severing of peaceful relations with Turkey. An expedition to Moldavia in 1620 under the leadership of Hetman Żółkiewski was unsuccessful in a battle with the Turks at Cecora and upon retreating was completely routed. The following year, the Polish army, with the decisive aid of the Cossacks, resisted the powerful Turkish forces, as a result of which peace was concluded.

The last phase of the war with Sweden was the most dangerous for the Commonwealth. In 1626, the Swedes seized the coastal part of Royal Prussia (apart from Gdańsk) and, despite the fact that the Polish forces scored several victories (including a naval victory in 1627 near Oliwa), they were not successful in repelling the invaders. The war ended in 1629 with a truce signed in Altmark. Under the terms of the truce the Swedes retained the larger part of Livonia, left troops in several strongholds on the Polish seacoast, and also obtained the right to collect customs duty in Gdańsk, which weighed heavily on Polish trade.

After the truce of Yam Zapolsky (1582), the territories of the Polish Commonwealth comprised about 815,000 sq. km. The conquests of Sigismund III in the East, before the losses in Livonia, increased this area to 990,000 sq. km. In the early 17th century, the population of the Commonwealth numbered 10—11 million inhabitants, of whom about 40 per cent were Polish.

The continued growth of manorial serf farms caused an increase in the burden on the peasants and their further impoverishment, which in turn limited demand for the products of urban craftsmen. Smaller towns were affected by this earlier, while the situation of larger centres which went in for luxury articles and foreign trade was still favourable in the first half of the 17th century. The large and prosperous town of Gdańsk, which enjoyed extensive economic and political privileges and even conducted its own foreign policy, occupied an exceptional position among the towns of the Commonwealth. Many representatives of the Catholic Church, above all the famous preacher and author Piotr Skarga, demanded an improvement of the peasants' lot.

In this period, increasing numbers of the gentry, some so impoverished as to be propertyless, became economically dependent on the magnates, who, as a result, had a stronger influence in the local diets and the Seym. The most powerful were the "little kings" of the Ukrainian marchlands, the owners of large latifundia. Magnates maintained their own armies and from the beginning of the 17th century, some of them waged private wars among themselves. At the same time, unpaid soldiers of the Commonwealth looted the countryside. The gradual limitation of royal prerogatives strengthened the Seym's role as the supreme authority in the state. Although the Chamber of Deputies acquired more importance than the Senate, this gave only the appearance of a further expansion of gentry democracy. In reality it amounted to an oligarchy of the magnates. Local diets, whose charters limited the power of the deputies, grew in significance, and since the tendency to demand unanimity increased at the end of the 16th century, some Seyms ended their sessions without passing any resolutions.

Initially the advocates of the Counter-Reformation declared themselves in favour of strengthening royal authority. However after Zebrzydowski's rebellion they went over to the camp of the defenders of "golden freedom". Following its successes, Catholicism became less and less tolerant. Persecution was directed chiefly against the Arians; the Arian Academy and printing house in Raków, renowned all over Europe, were closed down in 1638. The Polish Counter-Reformation was, however, not marked by the bloody intolerance which triumphed in the countries of western Europe, particularly Catholic Spain and Protestant England. Till the mid-17th century, the Polish Commonwealth continued to be an asylum for numerous foreigners fleeing from religious persecution in their own countries.

Jesuit schools played a decisive role in the education of the children of the gentry. Stephen Báthory raised the Jesuit College in Vilna (1578) to the level of an academy, and Jan Zamoyski established his own academy in Zamość (1595).

The style of dress, which emerged in the late 16th century and survived until the 18th century, was oriental in character and contained Turkish and even Persian motifs. An indispensable part of the gentry's attire and a symbol of membership of the ruling estate was a curved sabre, also of oriental origin. The whole costume, sumptuously adorned with silk belts, gold, pearls and precious stones, aroused admiration in western Europe. Though this Polish dress was essentially for the gentry, burghers and rich peasants attempted to imitate it both in style and colourfulness.

Magnate residences and gentry manor-houses were decorated with a multitude of Persian and Turkish tapestries, or Polish-made carpets recalling eastern patterns. Decorative arts were marked by foreign influences (for example Italian models in pottery and Dutch ones in tiled fire-places). Like the other fields of art, architecture, in which various south and north European elements were mixed, showed the influence of late Renaissance, Mannerism and early Baroque. The numerous residences, which combined sumptuousness with a defence capability, constituted an outward expression of the might of their owners who exerted an immense influence on the state and its policy.

The leading patrons of art were the Vasas — Sigismund III who moved his residence from Cracow to Warsaw, which now became the new capital, and his son, Ladislaus IV.

The newly-elected king, an able and educated man, was, unlike his father, popular among the mass of the gentry, although this popularity decreased as time went on. With the help of a group of enlightened magnates, such as Chancellor Jerzy Ossoliński, he tried to bring about internal state reforms but these attempts failed against strong opposition. Moreover, the king's impatience and lack of consistency also contributed to his failure. Ladislaus IV conducted a fairly flexible foreign policy, and relations with the Habsburgs were not as close as during the rule of Sigismund III.

At the beginning of his reign, Ladislaus IV had to wage war against Muscovy, whose armies were besieging Smolensk (1632). A relief force commanded by the king forced the Russian army to capitulate and led to the peace treaty of Polanowo (1634), which confirmed the possessions of both states gained under the Deulino Truce. It was then that Ladislaus IV renounced his title of Tsar and all claims to the throne of Muscovy. At the same time, following the repulse of an invading force of Tartars and Turks at Podolia in 1633, Polish-Turkish peace was restored.

The king, who was preparing a renewal of the war with Sweden, created a navy and built fortifications on the Hel peninsula; but the opposition of the magnates and gentry, who feared a strengthening of royal authority, prevented the declaration of war. As a result of the new truce, signed in Stumsdorf in 1635, the Swedes withdrew their forces from the strongholds in Polish ports and renounced the right to collect customs duties in Gdańsk.

Encouraged by Venetian, Papal and Imperial diplomacy, Ladislaus IV planned a major expedition against Turkey in order to liberate the Balkan peoples and conquer Constantinople. These projects were decisively rejected by the Seym in 1646 and 1647. This disappointed Cossack aspirations to participate in a war against Turkey and contributed to the outbreak of rebellion in the Ukraine.

It was the aim of the borderland magnates to limit the number of free or "registered" Cossacks who were in the pay of the Commonwealth and to reduce the remainder, who constituted the majority, to serfdom. This was the main cause of repeated Cossack uprisings, which were supported by the masses of Ruthenian peasants. The banner under which the Cossacks fought the Poles was the defence of the Orthodox faith, even though the Church hierarchy was re-established in 1620, and later officially legalized. A great Cossack uprising, under the leadership of

Bohdan Chmielnicki, broke out in 1648. Ladislaus' death at this time complicated the situation even further.

Magnate Rivalry and the Crisis of Sovereignty

John Casimir, brother of the deceased king, became his successor and also married the widowed Queen, Marie-Louise of the French ducal family of Gonzague. The queen, who was superior to the king in ability and strength of character, had a strong influence on the government.

Before the election of John Casimir, the Cossacks, aided by the Tartars, defeated the Polish army at Żółte Wody and at Korsun, and scored a victory over the mass levies at Pilavtse. The uprising embraced almost the entire Ruthenian population of the Ukrainian territories of the Commonwealth, where the Cossacks began to form their own state. The early attempts of the king and Chancellor Ossoliński to end the conflict on conciliatory terms yielded no results. Only in 1649, after the heroic defence of Zbarazh, which was besieged by Cossacks and Tartars, and the inconclusive battle of Zborów, an agreement was concluded under which the Poles were forced to make a number of concessions and to recognize the rule of Hetman Chmielnicki in the Ukraine. In 1651 the war was resumed. The victory of the Polish army over the Cossack and Tartar forces in a large-scale three-day battle at Berestechko ended in a new agreement signed at Byelaya Tserkov which was not as favourable to the Cossacks. Later renewed hostilities in the bloody battle of Batoh resulted in a new agreement at Żwaniec in 1653, which restored the provisions of the Zborów Agreement.

Chmielnicki sought the support of other countries and finally received it from Russia. Under the terms of the Pereyaslav Treaty of 1654 the Ukraine came under the rule of the Tsar of Muscovy. The war over the Ukraine, during which the Russians occupied almost the entire Grand Duchy of Lithuania, ended in a truce, signed in 1656; Muscovy did not wish to facilitate Swedish victory by continuing hostilities.

The Swedish King, Charles X Gustavus, in a bid to conquer the Baltic coast, invaded Poland in the summer of 1655. Exhausted by several years of war and unprepared for defence, Poland's situation was made even worse by the passivity and treachery of the magnates, who were opposed to John Casimir.

The *levée en masse* of Great Poland, led by Krzysztof Opaliński, capitulated in Ujście, and Janusz and Bogusław Radziwiłł surrendered Lithuania to the Swedes at Kiejdany. The gentry, who followed the example of the magnates, recognized the authority of Charles Gustavus at the local diets. After a few battles, the royal army surrendered and John Casimir took refuge in Silesia. Towards the end of 1655, the Swedish "Deluge" poured over almost all those territories of the Commonwealth which were not already occupied by Russians or Cossacks.

Looting and acts of violence on the part of the Protestant invaders soon provoked armed opposition among peasants, burghers and gentry in various parts of the country. The victorious defence of the monastery at Jasna Góra near Częstochowa resounded throughout the country. Upon his return to Poland, John Casimir was acclaimed by almost all the Poles who had formerly supported Sweden, while Stefan Czarniecki harassed the enemy by waging partisan warfare.

In 1656, Charles Gustavus obtained the help of the Elector of Brandenburg, Frederick William (known as the "Great Elector"), but his temporary successes did not improve the Swedes' military situation. Charles Gustavus brought about a treaty which envisaged the partition of the Commonwealth among Sweden, Brandenburg, Transylvania and the Cossacks. Moreover, Bogusław Radziwiłł was to obtain part of Lithuania as an independent duchy. The indirect result of this agreement was the destructive invasion of Poland by György Rákóczy, Duke of Transylvania (1657). It was then that Austria and Denmark entered the war against Sweden. The Elector of Brandenburg abandoned Charles Gustavus, but in return Poland had to conclude the treaty of Welawa in the autumn of 1657, by which John Casimir recognized the sovereignty of Frederick William in Ducal Prussia. In 1660, through the mediation of the French, peace was signed with the Swedes at Oliwa whereby the Commonwealth regained its pre-war territories.

The "Deluge", which wrought enormous destruction in the country, was over, but on Poland's eastern borders war was raging once more. Chmielnicki's successor, Jan Wyhowski, broke off the Treaty of Pereyaslav in 1658 and concluded an agreement with Poland in Hadziacz. This pact provided for the creation of an autonomous Duchy of Ruthenia within the Polish-Lithuanian State. The overwhelming majority of Ukrainians, however, were opposed to this agreement with the Commonwealth.

As a result, Polish-Russian hostilities flared up anew. The truce of Andruszów, signed in 1667, ended the war, with the territories of Smolensk, Chernigov and Novogrod Sieviezh, and part of the Ukraine on the left bank of the Dnieper, and Kiev going to Muscovy. These boundaries were later formally recognized by the Grzymułtowski peace of 1686. Military defeats accelerated Poland's internal crisis. For the first time, in 1652, a session of the Seym was broken off by a single deputy, or in other words by the *liberum veto*.

John Casimir and Marie-Louise sought to bring about constitutional reforms, to improve the nature of Seym debates, to introduce regular taxes, consolidate executive power and decide on the successor to the throne (the idea was to elect Henri Jules de Bourbon, the eldest son of the Great Condé). However, the opposition frustrated these plans. When its leader, Hetman (also Marshal) Jerzy Lubomirski was sentenced to banishment, a rebellion broke out under his leadership (1665—66). While the royal faction was connected with the French court, the rebels had the tacit support of Vienna. Despite the rebels' later capitulation, the king's defeat in the battle of Mątwy ruled out the possibility of further reforms.

After the queen's death, John Casimir abdicated in 1668 and departed for France, where he died in 1672. Thus ended the Polish Vasa line, a continuation of the Jagiellon dynasty.

A proposal for choosing a native Pole, or a "Piast", was put forward during the election. Michael Korybut Wiśniowiecki, son of the famous scourage of the Cossacks, Duke Jeremi Wiśniowiecki, was elected king. However he proved unable to cope with his responsibilities. Incompetent and lacking political instincts, he relied on Austrian support, thus becoming a tool of the magnates. The magnate opposition led by Hetman John Sobieski, on the other hand, was French-oriented.

In 1672, the Sultan Mohammed IV invaded the Commonwealth. The mighty stronghold of Kamieniec Podolski fell under the Turkish onslaught, thus forcing the Poles to conclude the ignominious treaty of Buczacz by which Turkey occupied Podolia and the southern part of the Kiev region, and was to receive a yearly tribute. The following year Sobieski scored a splendid victory over the Turks at Chocim, but he did not recover the lost territory. The king's death and the Chocim victory enabled Hetman Sobieski to assume the throne.

John III Sobieski was not only a talented leader, but also a man

of intellect and a shrewd politician. His aim was permanent
peace with Turkey and the reconquest of the Duchy of Prussia
from Brandenburg. This campaign was to be supported by alliances with France (1675) and Sweden (1677). However, the
king soon had to give up these plans. The war with the Ottoman
Empire ended only temporarily in a truce in 1676, by which
Poland regained a small part of the Ukraine as far as the Dnieper. The danger of Turkish invasion still existed and, since the
majority of the gentry and the magnates were opposed to the
alliance with Sweden and France, John Sobieski had to change
his political plans and ally himself with the Habsburgs against
Turkey. In 1683, the Commonwealth concluded an alliance
with Austria. With a huge Turkish army standing at the gates
of Vienna, the Poles hastened to relieve the city. Sobieski as
commander-in-chief of the combined Christian forces scored
a magnificent victory over the forces of the Grand Vizier, Kara
Mustafa (12 September 1683). The Battle of Vienna, in which
Polish heavy cavalry played an important part, was the Commonwealth's last great military success. This victory halted Turkish expansion in Europe. In 1684, Poland joined the anti-
Turkish Holy League and continued the war, which outlasted
the reign of John III.

In his internal policies, Sobieski aimed at strengthening his
authority and restraining the lawlessness of the magnates, but
was unable to overcome magnate and gentry opposition, which
was fomented by the intrigues of foreign ambassadors. Dis-
couraged by these misfortunes, the king gradually lost over
the years his initial energy and independence.

After the death of John III, the struggle for the Polish throne,
in which Queen Marie-Casimire ("Marysieńka") also participated, ended with the victory of the Saxon Elector, Frederick Augustus of the Wettin dynasty, who was supported by Austria and
Russia. Supported by only a minority of the gentry, he succeeded over Prince Louis of Conti, the choice of the majority.
Crowned as Augustus II, he was called the Strong for his unusual
physical strength. During his reign, he attempted to introduce
a hereditary and absolute monarchy in Poland.

During the first years of the personal Polish-Saxon union, the
Commonwealth regained territory lost under the Buczacz
Treaty and, together with other countries, signed the peace of
Karlovci with the Turks in 1699.

As a Saxon Elector, Augustus II allied himself with Russia and

Denmark in the war against the Swedes (the Northern War, 1700—21). In 1702, Charles XII of Sweden invaded Poland and, although the majority of the gentry remained loyal to the king and formed the Confederation of Sandomierz in his defence, some support was given to the Swedes. In 1704, the opponents of King Augustus the Strong declared him deposed and elected a magnate, Stanislaus Leszczyński, in his place. Leszczyński, however, was completely dependent upon the Swedes. Poland now had two kings and two foreign protectors, for at the same time the supporters of the legal ruler concluded a treaty with Peter the Great, which permitted Russian forces to operate in Commonwealth territory. In 1706, as a result of the Swedish invasion of Saxony, Augustus II was forced to abdicate. He regained the Polish crown in 1709, after the defeat of Charles XII at Poltava.

The excesses of Saxon troops in Poland led to the formation of the Confederation of Tarnogród in 1715, which was unofficially supported by Russia. This Confederation was directed against the king, but constituted at the same time the last effort on the part of the middle gentry to regain the political influence they had lost to the magnates. The civil war ended with the compromise treaty of Warsaw (1716), which was concluded with Russian aid, and by the "Dumb" Seym, at which the deputies were not allowed to speak lest the session be suspended (1717).

The one-day "Dumb" Seym underlined Poland's dependence upon Russia, who was the guarantor of the gentry's "golden freedom". Although the 1717 reforms of the treasury and the army were not comprehensive enough, for half a century it was impossible fully to implement and continue them.

While the Commonwealth was ceasing to play an active role in the international arena and falling into a state of political anarchy, not only the tsarist empire, but also Brandenburg, which in 1701 was proclaimed a Prussian kingdom were growing in strength. The latter was harbouring a predatory interest in Polish territory, desiring to link its Prussian possessions with Brandenburg through the annexation of Royal Prussia and Great Poland. Plans for partitioning Poland originated not only in Berlin, but also at the court of the Polish king. Augustus II wished to strengthen his authority and ensure his son the succession to the throne, even at the price of mutilating the country, and thus did not hesitate to put forward schemes of partition to other rulers. Attempts to partition Poland at this time were not immediately implemented, mainly because Russia preferred to keep the boundaries of the Commonwealth intact. However, these three neighbouring powers agreed among themselves to preserve the prevailing system of government in Poland and thus ensure her political weakness. Following earlier bilateral agreements, Russia, Austria and Prussia concluded in 1732 a secret treaty concerning Poland, known as the alliance of the three Black Eagles, after the emblems of the three states. The economic crisis in Poland had begun even earlier, but it was deepened by the ravages of war: the destruction caused by military operations, looting by troops of various nationalities and epidemics. The task of reconstruction after the devastation of the mid-17th century was not easy, and several years later, when some successes could be noted, there were the renewed setbacks of the Northern War. With only a few exceptions, the towns declined and the rural economy which to a great extent was based on serf labour, experienced a serious crisis. The exploitation of the mass of serfs, who constituted two thirds of the country's population, provoked spontaneous outbreaks against the lords.

Theoretically, the Commonwealth was still a democracy of the gentry, but for all practical purposes government was in the hands of a small group of magnates. The basis of their power lay in the large latifundia, their own armies and a host of completely dependent impoverished gentry. Individual magnates, their families and entire coteries, vied among themselves for primacy in the provinces and in the country as a whole. The membership of these parties and their political orientation varied, but those in favour of strengthening the already very weak royal authority were always in the minority. The opposition could count on far greater support from the middle gentry, who resisted all constitutional changes. Both the court faction and the oppositional groups sought aid from foreign countries.

The magnates controlled the state administration and crown estates. Ministers chosen by the king held appointments for life and did not have to account for their actions. The most powerful were the commanders-in-chief (hetmans) whose political role rivalled that of the king. With increasing frequency the Seyms were broken off by the *liberum veto*, not only in the interests of Polish magnates, but also at the financial instigation of foreign powers. Along with the decline of the General Assembly there was an increase in the significance of local diets, which voted in favour of local taxes and recruited their own forces. The power of the provincial diets, which were dependent on local potentates, was considerably limited by the "Dumb Seym", which restricted their fiscal competence and took away their right to raise armies.

The licence of the magnates, whose influence extended to the Tribunals, resulted in the breakdown of government institutions. The Commonwealth fell prey to anarchy. The gentry believed that the existence of such a state and the inviolability of its frontiers was in the interests of the neighbouring powers.

What the gentry valued above all was their "golden freedom", which was to be safeguarded by such inviolable rights as the tradition of free election and the *liberum veto*. The principle of the equality of all members of the gentry also belonged to these privileges. The more actual differences increased, the greater the stress laid on the semblance of equality (e.g. the refusal to acknowledge the aristocratic titles of old Lithuanian and Ruthenian ducal families). However in the 18th century an increasing number of magnate families received the title of count from the Emperor or the Pope.

The notion took shape among the gentry that the political structure of the Commonwealth was superior to that of other countries. National megalomania was connected with the self-glorification of the gentry estate as the core of a "gentry nation" and with xenophobia based on the conviction that all things alien might prove harmful to the national system and mores and in particular that the scourge of "tyranny" might infiltrate into the country.

This political ideology, as well as the entire gentry culture of the times, was known as Sarmatism. Though its roots went back to an earlier period, it reached its fullest expression in the second half of the 17th century. Its influence can be seen in the life-style of the gentry, which was characterized by conservatism and traditionalism, in their predilection for holding diets, making raids on their neighbours' estates and, above all, in feasting. The Baroque fondness for pomp contrasted sharply with the poverty and neglect of towns and villages. The Sarmatian predilection for oriental styles gave Polish Baroque literature and art its distinctive flavour. In architecture and art in particular it led to a peculiar mixture of western luxury and eastern colourfulness.

In the second half of the 17th century, there was an upsurge of intolerance and religious fanaticism in Poland, manifested in repressions against the Arians, then known as Socinians, who were banished from Poland by the Seym of 1658 (the Socinians had a considerable influence upon the development of western European philosophical and religious thought). The Seym of 1733 barred dissenters from holding public offices. The victorious Counter-Reformation placed the adherents of other faiths beyond the pale and insisted that every Pole be a Catholic. It was a general conviction of the time that the Commonwealth fulfilled a special mission as the "bulwark of Christianity", although since 1699 (the peace of Karlovci) this view had lost its basis in reality.

The victory of the Counter-Reformation and Sarmatism meant a decline in intellectual life in Poland, whose links with the culture of other countries became seriously weakened. Nonetheless, Polish cultural influence could be felt in Moldavia and Russia until the end of the 17th century.

A struggle for the Polish throne ensued after the death of Augustus II. In 1733, the majority of electors voted for Stanislaus Leszczyński, whose popularity had increased in Poland after the Northern War and who had French support (his daughter, Maria, was the wife of Louis XV). This attempt at defying the neighbouring powers was defeated by the armed intervention of Russia, who supported the minority favourite, the son of the late king. Leszczyński was forced to take refuge in Gdańsk, where he survived a siege by the tsarist armies. Later, however, he left for France and in 1736, renounced his right of succession in return for the right to rule for life over the Duchy of Lorraine (he died in 1766). Augustus III became king of Poland.

In contrast to his father, Augustus III proved to be an exceptionally incompetent ruler. He resided in Saxony and took no interest in Poland which the Saxon minister, Heinrich Brühl, governed on his behalf. During his reign only one Seym passed any resolutions; all others were broken off. During the Seven Years' War (1756—63), which was waged between Prussia, allied with Britain, and a coalition of Austria, Russia, France, Sweden and the majority of German states, the Commonwealth became a regroupment area for the fighting armies of Russia, Prussia and Austria.

Reform of the state was advocated by the Czartoryskis (known simply as the family) and their supporters among the gentry. In 1762—63 the Czartoryskis, supported by Russia, were preparing a *coup d'état* which was to enable the reform of the state system, however Catherine II postponed her intervention until the death of Augustus III.

The Saxon period saw the greatest decline of the Commonwealth, but the forces of change were already emerging. The lengthy period of peace favoured reconstruction and the economy began to improve, though slowly. A few great landowners commuted serf labour to money rents in order to stimulate manorial and peasant farming.

Publicists put forward projects of political reform, especially the abolition or limitation of the *liberum veto*. The most mature programme of improvements was introduced by a Piarist, Stanisław Konarski, in a work entitled *A Way to Effective Counsels* (*O skutecznym rad sposobie*, 1760—63). Earlier, he had initiated the modernization of the educational system by founding the *Collegium Nobilium* (Gentry College) in Warsaw in 1740. Here young men were to be educated in a patriotic and public spirit, for active participation in the political life of the country. His novel programme was later adopted by all Piarist and Jesuit schools. Scholarship revived after a period of stagnation and found patrons in the brothers Józef and Andrzej Załuski, who founded the first public library in Warsaw, one of the first and largest libraries in the world (1747). Intellectual change was encouraged by the ideas of the Enlightenment, which came to Poland from the West.

Reforms and the Downfall of the Commonwealth

The reign of Stanislaus Augustus Poniatowski was a period of tragic struggle for the rebirth and independence of Poland, a period of great achievements in the life of the nation, which nevertheless ended with the collapse of the State.

During the interregnum period (1763—64), armed Russian intervention encouraged by Prussia, enabled the supporters of the Czartoryski family to defeat their opponents. Stanislaus Augustus Poniatowski, the protégé of Catherine II and a member of the "Family", was elected king. His aim was to introduce reforms which would remove the most obvious disadvantages of the system of magnate oligarchy and help Poland out of its economic and cultural backwardness. While accepting Russian influence, he aspired to maximum independence in internal affairs.

The Convocation Seym was transformed into a General Confederation which made it possible to pass resolutions by a majority vote. In the years 1764—66, some proposals put forward by the Czartoryskis were put into effect, such as the establishment of fiscal and military commissions, which limited the licence of treasurers and hetmans, and the Treasury's revenues were increased. However, when the plan to curtail the *liberum veto* was introduced, Russia and Prussia demanded that the Convocation Confederation be dissolved and equality be granted to dissenters.

In 1767, under the protection of Russian troops, two dissident Confederations were established: a Lithuanian one at Słuck and a Polish one at Toruń. Under the inspiration of Repnin, Catherine's ambassador, a General Confederation was formed at Radom a few months later. In defence of the former government and the privileged position of Catholicism, it drew together the conservative opposition which demanded the abolition of all reforms and the dethronement of the king. Catherine II, however, disappointed the hopes of the Radom confederates. The Seym was forced to grant almost complete equal rights to dissenters, reforms of the executive arm were retained and Stanislaus Augustus, though humiliated, retained the Polish throne. During this Seym Russia's guarantee of cardinal rights was reaffirmed.

The frustrated hopes of the Radom confederates and Repnin's acts of violence resulted in the formation of the Confederation of Bar (1768—72). Organized at Bar in the Podolia region, the Confederation embraced all the provinces of the Commonwealth. It was an armed movement of the gentry against the king, the dissenters and Russia and in defence of class privileges, the Catholic religion and national independence. The gentry's guerrilla forces were opposed by tsarist troops and, in part, by the royal army. One of the talented Bar commanders was Casimir Pulaski, who later participated in the American War of Independence. The Confederation was led by the magnates, who were both quarrelsome and politically incompetent. Preceded by the proclamation of an interregnum, an attempt to kidnap Stanislaus Augustus failed (1771). In support of the Confederation, Turkey declared war on Russia (1768), and France sent instructors to Poland; but nothing was able to save the movement from defeat.

The Confederation of Bar, which linked resistance to constitutional reforms with the defence of independence, contributed to the growth of the gentry's political independence. The immediate results of the four-year civil war were catastrophic. It devastated the country, which was beginning to emerge from its decline, and gave the neighbouring powers a pretext for undertaking the first partition of Poland.

Prussia took advantage of Russia's being involved in a war with Turkey and induced her to agree to Poland's partition. In 1772, Austria joined the alliance and treaties of partition were signed. Prussia occupied Royal Prussia and Warmia, excluding Gdańsk and Toruń, and a stretch of Great Poland and Kuyawy on the Noteć River (36,000 sq. km.) — the smallest part in terms of area and population but the most important economically and politically. Austria received the most populated areas: southern Little Poland and almost all of Red Ruthenia, jointly known as Galicia (83,000 sq. km.). Russia occupied the extensive, but least significant area: Polish Livonia and part of Byelorussia up to the Dvina and Dnieper Rivers (92,000 sq. km.).

Altogether the Commonwealth lost 29 per cent of its former territory, which encompassed 733,000 sq. km., and about 35 per cent of its 12—14 million inhabitants. The Seym was forced to cede these territories formally in 1773.

In 1775, the partition Seym established a new system of government for the Commonwealth. The country would be ruled by a Permanent Council, composed of 18 senators and 18 representatives of the gentry, grouped into five ministerial departments, and presided over by the king. Stanislaus Augustus took advantage of Russian protection in order to safeguard Poland from further Prussian and Austrian annexations. On the other hand, however, St. Petersburg hindered the royal party's efforts at emancipation with the aid of the magnate opposition, which paralyzed reform movements even after 1780, when tsarist armies no longer occupied Poland. In 1776—78, the king undertook an attempt at peasant and urban reforms under the pretext of codification of the law, prepared under the guidance of Andrzej Zamoyski. This met with the stout resistance of Stackelberg, the Russian ambassador, the Papal nuncio and the gentry. Stanislaus Augustus also hoped to win Russian assent to an expansion of the army and a strengthening of the royal authority in exchange for Polish support in the war against Turkey. These hopes were dashed by Catherine II at a meeting with the Polish king at Kaniów in 1787. After the first partition, despite Russian opposition and the Prussian stranglehold on Polish Baltic trade, the Commonwealth recovered economically, reformed the treasury and administration, and established the nucleus of a modern army and an armaments industry. Officers were trained at the *Szkoła Rycerska* (Knights' School) founded by Stanislaus Augustus in 1765.

The abolition of internal customs duties and tolls, the establishment of general customs duties, the standardization of weights and measures and the establishment of Public Order Commissions for royal towns played an important role in the development of the cities. Noteworthy was the intense growth of the capital city of Warsaw, where new social groups as well as forms of economic (manufacturing, banking) and cultural life were beginning to emerge. The ideas of the Enlightenment had an important influence on changes taking place in Poland, especially on the country's cultural development. They also laid the foundations for the growth of a modern nation which encompassed not only the gentry, but all the estates. A leading role in this process was played by the intelligentsia, then beginning to emerge as a social group.

In 1773 the Seym established a National Education Commission which received the property of the Jesuit Order after the latter's abrogation by the Pope. This commission was the first state education authority in Europe to have the status of a separate ministry. The reform of the universities in Cracow and Vilna led to a development of mathematical and scientific research which largely closed the gap between Poland and the countries of western Europe. In Warsaw, where periodicals popularizing learning began to appear, it was mainly the humanities which developed. Both scientists and men of letters were advocates not only of cultural, but also of social and political progress. The most prominent writers of the period were Ignacy Krasicki, Stanisław Trembecki and Adam Naruszewicz (famous both as a poet and a historian). A Polish national theatre was born, thanks mainly to the efforts of Wojciech Bogusławski. Even earlier, Stanisław Konarski had fought for the purity of the Polish language which in the manner of the Baroque was thickly larded with Latin phrases. In the second half of the 18th century the works of outstanding writers set an example of natural and effective Polish which at that time also became the language of science. The patronage of the magnates and also of the king, whose enthusiasm for the arts decisively influenced the kind of art which flourished in his circle, continued to play an important role in cultural development (the Stanislaus Augustus style in architecture was a mixture of Italian Baroque and French Classicism). Despite its drawing on foreign patterns Polish art of this period still evolved its own national features. The discord between Russia and Prussia, which deepened during Russia's and Austria's war with Turkey (1787), gave the Commonwealth a convenient opportunity to free herself from Russia's guarantee. Prussia, which wanted to obtain more Polish territories peacefully in return for Poland's eventual recovery of Galicia from Austria, was interested in an alliance with Poland and a reduction of Russian influence in Warsaw.

In October 1788 there met in Warsaw a seym which came to be known as the Four-Year or Great Seym (from 1790 the number of its members was doubled), convened by Marshals (Speakers) Stanisław Małachowski and Kazimierz Nestor Sapieha. Right at the start an increase in the size of the army was voted and the evacuation of tsarist troops, which still remained in Poland, was demanded. The Permanent Council which Russia had imposed, was abolished. The army was to have been increased from under 20,000 to 100,000 men. It transpired, however, that despite a considerable increase in taxes, the highest figure that could be fixed was 65,000.

Resolutions rejecting Russian protection and calling for reforms emanated from the Patriotic Party, represented by the Seym majority led by Ignacy Potocki. The works of Stanisław Staszic and the publicistic writings of the outstanding statesman, Hugo Kołłątaj, and the writers gathered around him in the group known as "Kołłątaj's Forge", played an important part in uniting the supporters of Seym reforms, and especially in moulding public opinion. The Seym opposition, inspired by Russia, was headed by Hetman Franciszek Ksawery Branicki. At first, the king intended to introduce reforms without severing relations with Russia. By collaborating with the Patriotic Party, he finally accepted the latter's Prussian orientation and in 1790 concluded a treaty with Prussia.

Two resolutions of March and April 1791, concerning the reorganization of local diets and municipal government, preceded the Constitution of May Third, the greatest accomplishment of the Four-Year Seym. This Constitution was the second in the world, after that of the United States, to formulate principles of government in written form. Under the pressure of Warsaw patriotic opinion, the Seym shortened the procedure of passing the Constitution. The Constitution of May Third was the result of a compromise between the king, who had made a draft of the statute, and the leaders of the patriotic party. The Constitution, removing the basic faults of the former political system, such as the *liberum veto* and free election, considerably strengthened the power of the state. It made the throne hereditary, created a government in the form of the "Guardians of the Law" (the king, the primate and five ministers), limited the influence of the magnates, extended the rights of the burghers, and declared legal and government protection for the peasants. The Constitution was an attempt at introducing a parliamentary monarchy and, in accordance with the aims of its creators, it was intended as a starting point for further constitutional transformations. The Four-Year Seym's final year was spent in developing and modifying the provisions of the Constitution.

In the meantime, the approaching end of the war with Turkey moved the Empress Catherine not only to restore her protectorate in Poland, but also to abolish the reforms with the help of the conservative magnates. On 18 May 1792, a large Russian army crossed the borders of the Commonwealth. Simultaneously, an Act of Confederation, in defence of the gentry's violated "golden freedom" (the document had been signed earlier in St. Petersburg), was officially proclaimed in the border town of Targowica. Szczęsny Potocki became marshal of the Confederation.

Prussia failed to honour her alliance, and the Polish army was unable to stand up to the Russian army. The king and the leaders of the constitutional party did not believe in the effectiveness of opposition and the king ordered the troops to withdraw. After several battles and Catherine II's rejection of conciliatory proposals made by Stanislaus Augustus, the war ended with the king's capitulation and his accession to the Confederation of Targowica. The Targowica faction gained control of the country and banned all reforms.

On 23 January 1793, in St. Petersburg, Prussia concluded a second treaty with Russia for the partition of Poland whereby she annexed Gdańsk, Toruń, Great Poland and part of Mazovia and Kuyawy (57,000 sq. km.). Russia took the Ukrainian and Byelorussian territory east of the line Druia-Pinsk-Kamieniec Podolski (250,000 sq. km.). Austria did not take part in this partition.

The last Seym of the Commonwealth, which met in 1793 in Grodno, was forced to sanction these territorial losses, re-introduce the "cardinal" rights, and re-establish the Permanent Council, retaining only a few of the reforms of the Four-Year Seym. The second partition and Russian occupation intensified social ferment in what remained of the country and led to a conspiracy which was joined by patriots in emigration, who sought contacts with revolutionary France. After an acceleration in the reduction of the Polish army had been ordered and the conspirators in Warsaw arrested, insurrection broke out, its first act being the march of Madaliński's brigade from Ostrołęka to Cracow on 12 March 1794. General Tadeusz Kościuszko, a former participant in the American War of Independence and the war in defence of the Constitution of May Third, and an honorary citizen of France, proclaimed the act of insurrection in Cracow's Market Place and took the oath as Supreme Commander (24 March 1794). His victory at Racławice (4 April), in which peasant scythebearers played an important role, had wide repercussions. The Warsaw populace and soldiers, led by the cobbler Jan Kiliński, defeated the strongest Russian regiment in the country (17/18 April). A few days later, Jakub Jasiński, standing at the head of the army and supported by the populace, disarmed the Russian garrison in Vilna.

After his defeat at Szczekociny (6 June), Kościuszko retreated to Warsaw, which was holding out against a siege by Prussian and Russian armies (July-September). Insurrection broke out in Great Poland in August and was supported by an expeditionary force led by General Jan Henryk Dąbrowski. Meanwhile Cracow had capitulated in June, and in August Vilna fell.

On hearing of the approach of fresh Russian forces from the Ukraine, Kościuszko, who wanted to prevent the enemy's armies from linking up, attacked Fersen's corps at Maciejowice. He was, however, defeated and taken prisoner (10 October). He was replaced as commander-in-chief by Tomasz Wawrzecki. On 4 November the Russian army under Suvorov captured Praga, the right bank suburb of Warsaw and proceeded to slaughter the civilian population. Several days later Warsaw capitulated without offering any resistance. Part of the insurgent army retreated to the south. On 16 November the army became dispersed and Wawrzecki was taken prisoner. This marked the end of the Kościuszko Insurrection.

The insurrection did not formally abolish royal power, but

it did suspend it. In an attempt to improve the peasants' situation and encourage them to participate in the insurrection, Kościuszko issued the Połaniec Manifesto, which abolished serfdom and lowered labour dues (7 May 1794). The populace of Warsaw, inspired by radical Polish Jacobins, forced the leaders of the insurrection to take more decisive action and, faced with the latter's inaction, itself punished traitors (May-June). The Kościuszko Insurrection counted on aid from revolutionary France, which never came. On the other hand it considerably helped the situation of the French army by tying up the forces of the Revolution's enemies. Projects for a third partition, this time completely eliminating the Polish state, crystallized during the quelling of the insurrection. Bargaining among the powers involved lasted a year, and the third treaty of partition was concluded on 24 October 1795. Austria occupied the territory as far as the Pilica, Vistula and Bug (47,000 sq. km.), Prussia the region from the Pilica to the Bug and Niemen (48,000 sq. km.), while the remainder (120,000 sq. km.) went to Russia.

On 25 November 1795, Stanislaus Augustus was forced to abdicate (he died in 1798 in St. Petersburg). The Polish Commonwealth disappeared from the map of Europe. While other governments were indifferent to the partition of Poland or even supported it, liberal and democratic public opinion in Europe and North America condemned it as contrary to the law of nations.

The partitioning of Poland occurred during a period when the state was beginning to lift itself out of decline, an effort which, however, came too late. Nevertheless the social and cultural changes during the Enlightenment continued to influence national life, despite political subjection, while the Constitution of May Third and the Kościuszko Insurrection became a permanent part of the patriotic tradition.

Henryk Rutkowski

The First Ten Years of Subjection and the Striving for Independence

After the abolition of the Polish state, the three partitioning powers counted on the rapid and complete assimilation of the divided territories. They introduced their own laws and administrative system, removed members of the Polish gentry and aristocracy from important administrative offices, enforced conscription and raised taxes. Prussia and Austria insisted on the Germanization of the state administration and education. They strengthened and expanded the centralized civil service, but maintained the gentry's privileged social and economic position and the inviolability of the basic feudal structure. Serfdom was consolidated in the Russian zone, but in the Prussian and Austrian zones the intervention of government officials in disputes between peasants and landowners helped to weaken it. Moreover, peasants on estates belonging to the treasury had their labour dues commuted to money rents. The most patriotic sections of society, which were to be found chiefly among the intelligentsia, the impoverished gentry and moderately wealthy middle class, placed their hopes for independence in a victory of revolutionary France over Russia. The radicals, on the other hand, desired more a general armed insurrection, along with progressive reforms. At the end of 1795, several leaders of the Kościuszko Insurrection organized a conspiracy in the Austrian and Russian zones (the so-called Lvov Centralization); one of the radicals, Franciszek Gorzkowski, even undertook an anti-feudal campaign among the peasants in Podlasie. The conspirators maintained close contacts with small emigré groups in France and with Tadeusz Kościuszko, who was freed by Tsar Paul I and resided in the United States and, after 1798, in Paris.

Thanks to the emigrés' efforts and the French government's need to reinforce the Franco-Italian armies, who were fighting against Austria in northern Italy, Polish patriots were able to establish a national army corps. On the basis of an agreement made in 1797 with the government of the Republic of Lombardy, General Jan Henryk Dąbrowski organized two legions (regiments) "to aid Lombardy", gaining by this same agreement a guarantee of their Polish character and the possibility of an armed return to Poland. These legions, which numbered 7,000—9,000 men, fought alongside French troops in battles against Austria and the feudal governments of the Iberian peninsula, but also helped to strengthen French domination in the years 1797—1800. On the other hand, the Polish Danube Legion, organized in 1799 by General Karol Kniaziewicz, fought with the French army in Germany. It distinguished itself by a brilliant attack in the battle of Hohenlinden (1800), which was a decisive factor in France's victory over the Second Coalition.

When France concluded peace treaties with her opponents, Polish hopes for the country's liberation with French aid suffered a severe setback.

Some of the more active Polish leaders now concentrated their efforts on furthering cultural and enonomic advance (for instance by establishing the Society of Friends of Learning in Warsaw, and by promoting education, research into Polish history and language, and the establishment of museum collections). The patriotic and progressive Enlightenment tradition was still alive at this time, and led to a new flowering of culture. The defence of the Polish language and the cultivation of a feeling of unity among Poles who lived in the respective partitions, established a basis for the formation of a modern nation.

The words of Stanisław Staszic, scholar and writer of the Enlightenment, remained alive: "Even a great nation may by defeated, but only a base one decays of its own accord".

In 1803—05, Adam Jerzy Czartoryski, a liberal Polish aristocrat who was a friend of Tsar Alexander, and Russia's Minister of Foreign Affairs, attempted to restore Poland's statehood through Russian help. The failure of his plans and new wars strengthened the pro-French orientation anew.

The Duchy of Warsaw (1807—13) was formed as a result of France's victories over Prussia and Russia in 1806—07 and the valiant efforts of the Polish people itself. It encompassed most of the territory of the Prussian zone and constituted the nearest thing to a Polish state, in regard to degree of independence and extent of territory, to emerge during the partition period, i.e. between 1795 and 1918. The Napoleonic Constitution of 1807 for the first time introduced the legal foundations of a bourgeois society into Poland. It abolished inequality between social estates, granted political rights to the landowning gentry, wealthy burghers, rent-paying peasants and the intelligentsia. It introduced the bourgeois principle of equal rights for all and abolished personal serfdom and peasant bondage to the soil, although the land used by the peasants was recognized to be the property of the landowners. The Duchy of Warsaw enjoyed the most modern civil law of the day in the shape of the Napoleonic *Code Civil*. All the hopes of Polish patriots in the three partition zones were concentrated in the Duchy of Warsaw. Many such Poles clandestinely crossed the frontiers to join the national army or Polish administration, in the expectation of the country's speedy and total liberation. The existence of the Duchy strengthened the conviction of a considerable section of society that a victorious struggle for independence and the liquidation of the partitions was possible, and at the same time provided Poles with a new model of society, state and administration. The Duchy constituted an immediate continuation of the great socio-political and economic changes initiated on a large scale in the latter half of the 18th century and pointed the way to the formation during the following decades of the foundations of a modern society and nation.

In 1809, in the battle of Raszyn, the young Polish army of the Duchy of Warsaw successfully stood up against the attacks of the strong Austrian army, which aimed at destroying the Duchy during the war with Napoleon. The commander-in-chief of the Polish army, Prince Józef Poniatowski, liberated a considerable part of the Austrian zone (including Cracow and Zamość), which was annexed by the Duchy under the terms of the Franco-Austrian peace treaty.

Napoleon's defeat in the War of 1812, and his final downfall in 1814—15, sealed the fate of the Duchy. At the Congress of Vienna in 1815, Prussia was assigned part of the area which had belonged to the Duchy of Warsaw (Toruń, Poznań and Bydgoszcz) and the district of Cracow was established as a "free and independent city", subject to the three partitioning powers (the so-called Commonwealth of Cracow). The remaining territory of the Duchy of Warsaw was allowed to preserve a measure of independence (its own Seym, government, army, treasury, laws and administration), and formed the Kingdom of Poland. It was firmly linked with the Russian Empire and subject to the rule of the tsar, one of whose titles was now "King of Poland". At the same time the Kingdom of Poland received a liberal constitution in 1815.

National Uprisings and the Abolition of the Feudal Order

After 1815 reactionary tendencies were strengthened in the policies of the governments of Russia, Austria and Prussia. They did not keep their promises of ensuring the development of "Polish nationality" (in education and administration); they persecuted all liberal thought and aspirations for progress and independence. Only in the Russian partition was the situation of the Poles somewhat different. The creation of the Kingdom of Poland by Tsar Alexander I, together with the large share of Poles in the administration and educational system of the western provinces of the Russian Empire, seemed to strengthen, and even extend, the Polish gains of previous years. But a mere four years later there arose a sharpening of antagonisms between the sovereign and the government of the Kingdom on the one hand and the prevailing desires and opinions of the people on the other. There was a rapid and decided growth of reactionary tendencies in the policy of the ruler. Alexander I (and later his successor, Nicholas I), made certain that his brother, the Grand Duke Constantine, who was commander-in-chief of the Polish army, and Novosiltsov, his personal representative in Warsaw, had a dominating influence in the government. They suppressed all signs of opposition in the press and the Seym, infringed the Kingdom's Constitution and persecuted secret youth socie ties (in 1822 the Panta Koina in Warsaw and in 1823 the Society of Philomats in Vilna). In 1826, they broke up the Patriotic Society, founded in 1819—21 by Major Walerian Łukasiński, which was the strongest of the underground organizations, having cells in all three partitions and maintaining contacts with western European and Russian revolutionaries (the Southern [Decembrist] Society). This led to increased opposition among the Polish population, while the Romantic literature and political thought of the time kept alive hopes for complete national liberation. A conspiracy formed by Piotr Wysocki at the end of 1828 in Warsaw's Infantry Officers' School, prepared for a national insurrection, to be strengthened by civilian conspirators.

Influenced by hopes arising out of the victorious revolution in France in July 1830 and the expected assistance of the British government, as well as fearing the collapse of the conspiracy through new arrests and especially through the tsar's dispatching of the Polish army against the revolutionary forces in France and Belgium, the conspirators gave the signal for the outbreak of an uprising. During the evening of 29 November 1830, they occupied key positions in the city, thanks to the support of the Warsaw populace and the capture of the Arsenal. This marked the beginning of the November Insurrection. The leadership of the movement was seized by conciliatory and conservative groups (General Józef Chłopicki, Prince Adam Jerzy Czartoryski). Unsure of victory, they vainly sought the aid of Britain, France or Austria, or a compromise with the tsar.

But patriotically oriented circles and the Left Wing of the Patriotic Society desired a genuine struggle for independence. Thanks to them, during the next few months the small Kingdom of Poland conducted a regular war with the greatest continental power of the day, Tsarist Russia. The rebel armies were able to delay the Russian offensive at the approaches to Warsaw in the battle of Grochów (1831) and even defeat part of the enemy's forces at Wawer, Dębe Wielkie and Iganie. In the spring, smaller rebel forces took up arms in the regions of Vilna, Żmudź and the Ukraine. However, the defeat at Ostrołęka, for which the commander-in-chief was responsible, weakened the insurgents and their will to fight. Warsaw capitulated after a two-day assault by the tsarist armies, and in the second half of September and beginning of October almost 40,000 rebels crossed the borders of Austria and Prussia. The capitulation of Modlin and Zamość marked the definitive collapse of the insurrection.

The November Insurrection, which was militarily the strongest of all the Polish national uprisings, strengthened patriotic sentiments and desires for independence. Volunteers and financial aid flowed in from the Austrian and Prussian zones and even from Silesia. News of the insurrection became an important stimulus in arousing national awareness in Mazuria and Silesia. The Insurrection ruled out the possibility of tsarist intervention against France or Belgium, which was then struggling to liberate itself, but did not receive any help from western governments.

Immediately after the collapse of the Insurrection, the numerous Poles who escaped abroad (the Great Emigration) undertook attempts to continue the struggle and work out new programmes of national liberation. The exiles settled in France, Britain, the United States and other countries of western Europe and America. In the coming years, this group also included the most prominent and most active leaders of the national movement, as well as writers, musicians and scientists. The vital, unhampered cultural life of the Emigration, the atmosphere of fervent patriotism and longing for home, of great political and ideological disputes, favoured cultural achievements and enabled Poland to make an important contribution to European culture at this time. There arose at that time many outstanding works of Romantic literature and music, and historical research became enriched. The latter was infused by the greatest Polish historian and outstanding emigré leader, Joachim Lelewel, with democratic tendencies (by making the people — the nation — and not the gentry or individuals, the subject of history) and a profound patriotism (a particular interest in the fate of the nation and especially aspirations to national freedom).

Art in the Romantic period as well as the social sciences, reflected the most important problems of the Polish nation in captivity. Music employed the motives and forms of folk compositions and the finest exponent of this style was Frédéric Chopin. Literature dealt with the problems of life under foreign rule. Polish Romantic literature was more preoccupied with national existence and the struggle for independence than that of any other European country.

The ideal of national liberation can be found in the works of Poland's three most famous poets — Adam Mickiewicz, Juliusz Słowacki and Zygmunt Krasiński — as well as in the intellectual, modern poetry of Cyprian Kamil Norwid. Their work contained at the same time universal human values: an understanding of the inevitability of the victory of progress, criticism of injustice, a defence of the rights — especially to freedom and justice — of nations, individual social groups and every human being.

Creative writing evolved in close connection with the buoyant political life of the Great Emigration, which at that time had particular significance. As a result of sharp conflicts, more modern political movements were formed and standpoints within the national movement became polarized.

The right wing was represented by the aristocratic and landowning camp of Adam Czartoryski, known as the Hôtel Lambert (after the name of the Czartoryski residence in Paris). Czartoryski wanted to attain liberation through the diplomacy and successes of the western powers, and put off "a properly timed insurrection" into the indefinite future. His aim was to establish a constitutional monarchy which would preserve the primacy of the aristocratic landowning classes, but as far as the peasant problem was concerned he merely appealed to the squires to introduce labour rents or to enfranchise their peasants. The Hôtel Lambert played an important role in keeping alive the Polish question in Europe, in promoting the national, cultural and intellectual life of the Emigration, arousing and strengthening national and independence aspirations among the Balkan Slavs and Rumanians, and in interesting western European governments and public opinion in the latter.

The claim to hegemony among the liberal and conservative leaders of the Hôtel Lambert faction met with the opposition of the democratic camp. This group established more cohesive organizations and socio-political programmes and had the support of the majority of exiles, although it was weakened by internal divisions. At first the moderate democratic groups, which formed the movement's right wing (led by the prominent historian, Joachim Lelewel), had the advantage. Their overtly conciliatory position, however, provoked the dissent of the radicals who established the Polish Democratic Society (1832—62), which became the strongest emigré grouping (it numbered over 2,000 members). Its programme, defined in the *Great Manifesto* (1836), postulated the liberation of Poland by means of a general national insurrection, with the participation of the popular masses and under the leadership of the most patriotic sections of the gentry and intelligentsia. On the day of the insurrection, the peasants would be granted full property rights without compensation to the landowners. In a liberated Poland, the Polish Democratic Society wanted to enforce democratic-republican reforms, but in its attitude to private property it accepted a bourgeois structure. The principles of the *Great Manifesto* became the basic programme of democratic national liberation trends until 1863, but they also met with criticism from the most radical revolutionary forces.

Even while the *Great Manifesto* was being prepared, extreme left-wing, revolutionary democrats left the Society and formed the "Polish People in Emigration" (Communes of the Polish People of Grudziąż, Humań and Praga, 1835—46). This organization wanted to link the struggle for independence to the complete abolition of private property. In this way the victorious people was to overthrow exploitation and guarantee full democracy.

Democtratic groups entered into extensive alliances with revolutionaries in France, Germany, Italy, Britain and Russia, and often participated in demonstrations against despotism and national oppression. Above all, they attempted to influence Polish society in order to create a large-scale conspiracy which would lead to a speedy national insurrection.

In Poland, the failure of the November Insurrection at first weakened the nation's spirit and fighting capacity. The victorious tsar drastically limited the autonomy of the Kingdom of Poland (by abolishing the Seym and separate army, and reducing the separateness of the legal and administrative system), closed down Polish universities and abolished the Society of the Friends of Learning in Warsaw, and began a movement of Russification, especially in the western provinces of the Empire. Prussia and Austria, who closely collaborated with the tsar, also sharpened their anti-Polish campaign. The national movement, however, grew stronger, despite the ruthless repression by the partitioning powers. Some landowners and members of the intelligentsia (especially those in the Prussian zone), who were opposed to the insurrection, attempted to strengthen Polish national consciousness by establishing legal economic and cultural associations.

On the other hand, students, the impoverished gentry and the younger intelligentsia swelled the ranks of the underground movement in all three partitions. During the years 1832—39, it grew in strength mainly in the Commonwealth of Cracow and Galicia, but reached as far as the Kingdom of Poland and the Ukraine (the Szymon Konarski conspiracy). After 1840, the underground movement began to reach working class circles (the Union of Plebeians in Poznań) and even the peasantry (the Peasant Association founded by Father Piotr Ściegienny in the Kielce and Lublin regions), and the democratic programme of the Great Emigration gave them a revolutionary and democratic stamp. This movement called for the transformation of the future insurrection into a "people's war" (Henryk Kamieński), Russo-Polish revolutionary cooperation against the tsar, and the linking of the war for independence with a complete social revolution. The left-wing conspiracy represented by Edward Dembowski, an eminent philosopher and publicist, and remarkable organizer, aimed at an early outbreak of the insurrection in all three partitions. However, on the eve of the uprising in 1846, arrests in Lvov, Warsaw and above all in the Poznań area, broke up the main centres of the conspiracy and paralyzed the entire enterprise.

Short-lived armed struggles broke out in only a few parts of the country. A National Government was established in liberated Cracow and in a manifesto proclaimed the abolition of all caste and class privileges, the enfranchisement of the peasants and social care for the poor and incapacitated; it also promised land allotments to participants in the insurrection. The Cracow Uprising collapsed, but thanks to its radical principles, it became an important milestone in the Polish struggle for national liberation. It met with an enthusiastic reception on the part of the great majority of Polish emigrés and all democratic circles in Europe. The programme contained in the Manifesto of the National Government was assessed very highly by Marx and Engels as the most consistent solution of the agrarian question and liquidation of existing elements of feudalism, as a model of the skilful combination of national aims with a radical transformation of the social structure. Such a positive assessment of the movement was undoubtedly influenced by the activity of Edward Dembowski, the most outstanding revolutionary of the Polish national liberation movement. Dembowski — as secretary to the Dictator — contributed to the radicalization of the insurrectionary programme and made efforts to win over the broad masses of the people to active participation in the Uprising.

It was the peasants' attitude that decided the early failure of the insurrection. Only in a few areas (Miechów in the Kingdom and Chochołów in Galicia) did the rural population turn out against the partitioning powers. Oppressed by the landowners, illiterate Galician peasants assumed a distrustful and hostile attitude towards the "lords' uprising", and in Tarnów, Jasło, Sącz and Przemyśl, undertook their own armed uprising against the landowners and bailiffs. This spontaneous, unorganized peasant uprising ("the Galician slaughter") which was led by local leaders (the most noted was Jakub Szela), was quickly suppressed.

The failure of the national insurrection of 1846 caused a new wave of repression, sharpened the anti-Polish policies of the partitioning powers and resulted in the abolition of the Commonwealth of Cracow and its annexation to the Austrian zone (1846).

The aforementioned failures weakened the strength and independence of the Polish national liberation movement during the period of the great European revolutionary upheavals known as the "Springtime of Nations", in the years 1848—49. Revolutionary movements in France, Austria, Italy, Germany and Hungary brought a short-lived, though strong, outburst of sympathy for the Poles and their liberation aims, and this became an important element in the struggles against European reaction. In turn, the fate of the Polish question at this time depended in large measure upon the fate of the other European revolutionary and national liberation movements, the growth of which increased Polish hopes for liberation.

Poznań revolutionaries were the first to initiate a national movement, simultaneously with the outbreak of the revolution in Berlin. The National Committee (founded in Poznań in 1848) attempted to gain extensive autonomy for this province through an agreement with the new bourgeois government of Prussia.

At first, the Prussian government and king vaguely expressed their support; in this manner, they counted on winning the favour of the Poles and securing the victory of the Polish cause in the expected war against Russia over the unification of Germany. However, the authorities increasingly restricted their promised concessions and the generals provoked an armed conflict with the few and ill-prepared Polish detachments. In May, the Prussians definitely suppressed the Poznań Rising, and, in 1850—52, they forbade the functioning of the Polish League (founded in 1848); this was a large legal organization which strove to counter the threat to Polish national identity in Pomerania and the Poznań area.

Despite the final victory of the Prussian reactionaries, the "Springtime of Nations" brought a consolidation of the Polish national movements in the lands subject to Prussia and the political activation of the Polish inhabitants of Pomerania, Mazuria and Silesia. The peasants constituted an important, patriotic and self-sacrificing force in the Poznań Rising. The struggle of the common people in Silesia, Pomerania and Mazuria for the use of the Polish language in schools and offices initiated the process of national revival in these territories, which had undergone centuries of Germanization. In Gdańsk Pomerania and Silesia the Polish population elected Poles to the Prussian and German parliaments. Great activity and initiative was shown by the still numerically small Polish intelligentsia. In Pomerania Ignacy Łyskowski founded and published the paper *Szkółka Narodowa* (National Nursery), and in constitutional clubs in Mazuria people discussed, usually in Polish, current political problems. In the Bytom region of Silesia the village teachers Józef Lompa and Emanuel Smolka, together with the priest Father Józef Szafranek, created a strong centre of Polish national agitation. In Bytom a National Club and Polish reading room were organized. Silesians were made aware of their former links with Poland, and a mass struggle against Germanization was organized. Bowing to popular pressure, the authorities restored the use of the Polish language in elementary schools.

A strong Polish national movement led by moderate, liberal politicians also developed in the Austrian zone (especially Lvov and Cracow). Counting on the easy victory of revolutionary and liberation forces in Austria, they hoped to secure extensive autonomy and even the independence of the Austrian zone by peaceful means. At the same time they induced the landowners, to enfranchise the peasants, in order to win over the rural population for their movement. After short armed conflicts in Cracow and Lvov, provoked by the Austrians, the victorious reactionaries suppressed the Polish liberation movement. However, the permanent gains of this movement were the enfranchisement of the peasants, the growth of Polish collaboration with other nationalities of the Austro-Hungarian Empire and the beginnings of a Polish national movement and national revival in Cieszyn Silesia (belonging to Austria). In this last region an as yet small group of Polish intelligentsia (Paweł Stalmach, Andrzej Cinciała) founded the *Tygodnik Cieszyński* (Cieszyn Weekly) and a Polish reading room, patiently undertaking the work of making the local people conscious of their Polish origin.

Poles also participated in national liberation movements in many European countries, emphasizing the truth of the slogan "for our freedom and yours". In Italy, Adam Mickiewicz organized a small legion (1848), which fought for the liberation of Northern Italy from Austrian rule and defended the Republic of Rome; he also tried to persuade the Italians to form Slav legions in the joint struggle against Austria. In 1849, in Paris, he edited *La Tribune des Peuples* in cooperation with French, German, Russian, Italian and Spanish journalists, who professed democratic and revolutionary opinions. In 1848, several hundred Poles engaged in joint action with Rumanian revolutionists, who were fighting for thoroughgoing reforms and the unification of their native land; smaller groups participated in liberation battles in Italy, Vienna, Dresden, Baden and the Palatinate.

Polish valour and self-sacrifice were widely recognized. General Wojciech Chrzanowski was entrusted with the command of the Sardinian forces fighting against Austria (1849) and General Ludwik Mierosławski was put in command of the revolutionary armies in Sicily and Baden. Over 3,000 Poles (concentrated mainly in General Józef Wysocki's Polish legion) fought in the Hungarian Revolution (1848—49) against Austria and the interventionist army of the tsar; Generals Henryk Dembiński and

Józef Bem temporarily even held the position of commander-in-chief. General Józef Bem (who defended revolutionary Vienna in October 1848) gained special fame through his victories in Transylvania. The "Springtime of Nations" finally ended in the victory of the reactionary forces, which completely erased Polish hopes for an early liberation.

These hopes rose anew at the outbreak of the Crimean War, when Polish emigrés began to organize military formations to aid Turkey and Britain. The Paris Peace Treaty (1856) disappointed hopes that the war might spread to Polish territory.

However, the tsar's defeat in the Crimean War and Italy's success in forming a unified national government gave a new impetus to the struggle for national liberation. The crisis in the Russian Empire and the increase in revolutionary activity in Russia itself as well as peasant aspirations towards emancipation, created a favourable background for the struggle for social reforms, national concessions and even independence. As early as 1857—58, the first conspiratorial organizations of Polish students were formed in Kiev, Moscow and Warsaw. A group of officers, the majority of whom were Poles (Zygmunt Sierakowski, Jarosław Dąbrowski and others), were active in conspiracies at the General Staff Academy in St. Petersburg. In June 1860, secret student organizations in Warsaw initiated mass national demonstrations which aroused patriotic sentiment and the desire to fight for freedom. Making minimal concessions, the tsar bloodily crushed two of the strongest demonstrations in Warsaw in February and June 1861, thus indicating his refusal to grant greater autonomy to the Kingdom of Poland. Tsarist policy prevented the emergence of a strong conciliatory party among the Polish nobility and accelerated the growth and polarization of the underground movement. They also caused the unpopularity of Margrave Aleksander Wielopolski (since May 1862, chief of the civilian government of the Kingdom) who, at the price of minor concessions and limited progressive reforms, aspired to harmonious cooperation with the tsarist government.

In the years 1861—62, some democratic and revolutionary groups (known as "Reds") developed a large-scale, well-organized conspiratorial network in the three partition zones, directed by a Central National Committee. On the other hand, more moderate leaders among the landowners, bourgeoisie and intelligentsia ("Whites") established their own secret organization, headed by a National Directory. The former wanted an early outbreak of a national insurrection in order to secure complete independence and democratic political and social reforms (especially peasant affranchisement). The latter sought to direct the national movement towards further struggles by peaceful means and the accomplishment of moderate social reforms. Recognizing the Russian revolutionary movement as their fundamental ally in the future insurrection, the "Reds" entered into close cooperation with the Russian revolutionaries (the Land and Freedom organization) towards the end of 1862. The date settled for the uprising had to be abandoned owing to the extraordinary conscription ordered by Wielopolski in the middle of January 1863. The Central Committee, fearing the breakdown of the conspiracy and the weakening of the national movement as a result of the levy, advanced the outbreak of the January Insurrection. On 22 January 1863, it issued a Manifesto proclaiming itself the National Government and called the "Polish, Lithuanian and Russian nations" to arms against the tsar. By a special decree, it granted the peasants the right to own the land they cultivated, promised landowners compensation from treasury funds, and offered the landless peasants three *morga* (1 *morga* — 5,600 sq. m. — ed. note) of land in return for their participation in the insurrection. During the night of 22/23 January, the few detachments of poorly armed insurgents began fighting in various localities. In face of the overwhelming odds (Russian troops numbered 100,000—340,000), the war assumed the form of a partisan movement, especially in the regions of Kielce, Sandomierz, Lublin and Podlasie, which received financial aid and thousands of volunteers from the Austrian and Prussian zones. At the end of February, the insurrection also embraced Lithuania, Byelorussia and the Ukraine. At this moment the uprising disposed of an extraordinarily extensive secret organizational network which amounted almost to a complete State administration (central and local government, representatives from outside the partition, armed detachments, postal service, police, printing offices, arms production and distribution, and even a tax levy for insurrectionary purposes!).

The "Whites" joined the insurrection after a few weeks of fighting, desiring to weaken the radical tendencies of the movement, but also yielding to the pressure of patriotic sentiments and, above all, believing in the effective intervention of the western powers on behalf of the Polish cause. In the autumn of 1863, they withdrew from further participation in the insurrection (disappointed in their hopes for intervention), but enabled General Romuald Traugutt, one of the rebels, to assume dictatorial powers. Relying on "Red" policies, he undertook an energetic reorganization of the faltering rebel forces and ordered the thorough implementation of the affranchisement decree. By the first months of 1864, the tsarist government had defeated all partisan detachments and rebel organizations, and by issuing the emancipation decree on 2 March 1864, won over the peasants and prevented them from helping the insurgents. Traugutt and his closest associates were hanged on the slopes of the Warsaw Citadel; the defeat of Father Brzóska's forces in Podlasie in the autumn of 1864, definitively put an end to the uprising.

The heroic struggle of the Polish nation gained the warm sympathy and support of European revolutionaries and of public opinion. It is true that hopes of a strong revolutionary movement in Russia were disappointed, but several hundred Russians and Ukrainians (including Andrey Potebnia) abandoned the tsarist armies, and fought in or even commanded partisan detachments. In his newspaper *Kolokol* (The Bell), the great Russian democrat and publicist, Alexander Herzen, fully supported the Poles' just cause and Russo-Polish collaboration, despite the campaign of chauvinism unleashed by the tsarist government. Hungarian, French, Italian, German and Bohemian volunteers fought in the ranks of the insurrection, and meetings of British and French workers, organized in the summer of 1863 in support of the Polish cause, led to the foundation of the First International. On the other hand, the diplomatic intervention of France, Britain and Austria, initiated by Napoleon III, failed utterly, to the Poles' great disillusionment.

The failure of the largest and one of the most radical of Polish insurrections (15 months of fighting, about 1,200 skirmishes and 200,000 active rebels) brought in its train the total abolition of the autonomous Kingdom of Poland and a severe policy of Russification. On the other hand it also led to affranchisement reforms more favourable to the peasants than those introduced in neighbouring countries.

The national liberation movement of the years 1795—1864 ended in defeat, growing repression and denationalization policies. However, it greatly contributed to awakening Polish national awareness, to the political and patriotic activation of the intelligentsia, bourgeoisie, peasants and the newly-formed working class (the January Insurrection). It also accelerated social changes as a result of which the feudal structure was finally replaced by a capitalist one in the second half of the 19th century. These changes, in combination with the operation of the rich Polish culture and the impressive endurance and self-sacrifice of Polish society in the struggle for freedom, often became a stimulus for the national assimilation of non-Polish elements — especially among newcomers from Germany and the fairly numerous Jewish population of the towns and villages.

The fundamental stimulus for these changes came from eco nomic developments after the 1820's. Several important industrial centres grew up at this time in Upper Silesia, Cieszyn Silesia and the Kingdom of Poland (mining and metallurgical industries), in Łódź and Białystok (the textile industry), in Szczecin, Gdańsk and Elbląg (shipping) and in Poznań, Pomerania and the Kingdom of Poland (the food processing industry). The first railways were built linking Warsaw with Vienna and St. Petersburg, Silesia and Cracow with Berlin, and Poznań with Szczecin, and the significance of banking increased. At first large-scale manufactories replaced individual artisan production and the first factories using machinery made their appearance in the thirties and forties. The growth of large industrial companies strengthened the bourgeoisie and at the same time gave birth to a working class, which undertook sporadic and spontaneous strike action against exploitation (in 1824—30, there were strikes in Warsaw and Łódź, and in 1844 there were famous demonstrations of weavers in Silesia). In the Prussian and Russian zones, agrarian reforms replaced the three-field system by crop rotation, introduced the use of fertilizers and modern agricultural equipment and machinery, and the use of hired labour on manorial farms. The complete victory of capitalist relations became possible only after the abolition of serfdom and the affranchisement of the peasants (in the Prussian zone in 1811—23, in the Austrian zone in 1848, and in the Russian zone in 1864).

A factor unifying Polish society in the 19th century and to a large extent influencing public awareness and opinions, was the intensive development of a common culture linking all three partitions. Apart from the great writers and artists working in emigration, an important role was played in Poland itself by the music, based on folk motifs, of Stanisław Moniuszko, "father of the national opera", while the paintings of Jan Matejko, Juliusz Kossak and Artur Grottger provided a lesson in patriotic history for many generations to come. Cities played an ever increasing role in the creation and popularization of culture, as well as in general progress. Economic and administrative development favoured the growth of large planned urban centres. As far as the level of civilization, dress and customs were concerned, city life varied more and more from village life. Theatres, bookshops, printing-houses and newspapers were concentrated to an ever increasing degree in the large towns, which thus attracted painters, graphic artists, sculptors and musicians. Thus their influence on the development of literature and art steadily increased, and culture extended to reach ever wider strata of society, owing to the development of publishing, the press and education. The number of schools (especially in the Prussian zone) and universities also increased: apart from the existing universities of Cracow and Vilna, there were the University of Warsaw (1816—31), the Medical-Surgical Academy (1857—62), Warsaw's Main School (1862—69) and the Warsaw Conservatory and School of Fine Arts; illiterates however still constituted the overwhelming majority of the population. Despite unfavourable conditions and lack of government aid, scientific societies were organized and the humanities developed, while in the natural sciences Ignacy Domeyko (geologist and mineralogist) and Ignacy Łukasiewicz (who discovered a method for the distillation of crude oil and the kerosene lamp) won fame for themselves. Large collections of prints and manuscripts (the Krasiński Library in Warsaw, the Raczyński Library in Poznań, the Polish Library in Paris), and especially the Ossoliński National Institute in Lvov (also a publishing house), which was founded by Józef Maksymilian Ossoliński in 1817, fulfilled an important scientific and cultural role.

Socio-enonomic, political and cultural changes touched off a profound social metamorphosis and led to the birth of a modern nation. The growth of democratic and revolutionary tendencies in the national liberation movement restricted the political role of the gentry in Polish society. At the same time, it accelerated reforms which abolished the feudal structure and by the same token weakened the gentry's socio-economic position and caused the overthrow of social class divisions. Thanks to agrarian reforms, the peasants became an independent social class, and their awareness grew along with their independence. Jointly with other classes, they opposed the severe denationalization policies of the partitioning powers and kept up a long struggle in defence of their Polish language and Polish identity. In this manner, the common people became a vital, active part of the Polish nation, and in Silesia, Warmia, Mazuria and Pomerania, the only force which, together with a small group of local intellectuals, struggled to preserve the Polish character of their homeland. However, there was an increase in periodicals and literature intended for the more enlightened strata of the peasantry, which stimulated pride in Polish history and an awareness of belonging to the Polish nation; the common people now participated increasingly in the struggle for national liberation. The more sophisticated literature of the Romantic period, which was almost completely devoted to the liberation struggle, strengthened the national awareness of the upper and educated classes. Among them an increasing role was played by the intelligentsia and bourgeoisie, which grew in strength together with socio-economic changes. The younger intelligentsia, who were mainly responsible for the national culture of the time, brought about an awakening of national awareness and kept alive hopes for liberation.

Fundamental transformations were initiated in the Polish nation. The common people's national awareness found expression in a clinging to the native tongue and customs, while the sense of division between different social classes still occasionally hampered the formation of strong ties and a clearer sense of common interests. The process of the birth of a modern nation and national awareness was to be continued and deepened in the following decades.

Jerzy Skowronek

Polish Society after the January Insurrection

The collapse of the January Insurrection was an extremely important stage in the history of the Polish nation. It ended a period of struggle for national independence in which the dominant role had been played by the revolutionary section of the gentry, a period during which the latter constituted the nation's leading political force. Gradually, the relatively weak bourgeoisie, the peasant masses, and above all the proletariat, which was beginning to take shape at the time, began playing a role of increasing importance in political life.

Decrees issued by the insurrectionist National Government granting peasants ownership of the land they tilled, exercised an influence of fundamental importance on the subsequent development of Polish society. Despite the suppression of the Insurrection and the crushing of the well-organized and efficiently run Polish underground state, the decisions regarding the enfranchisement of the peasants, carried out at the time, determined once and for all the method of settling Poland's most important socio-political problem, apart from the restoration of independent statehood. Determined to benefit from these decisions, the tsar issued a ukase recognizing the enfranchisement decrees of the insurgent government. As a result, peasants in the Kingdom of Poland were granted land on much more favourable conditions than in any other part of the Russian Empire.

Enfranchisement of the peasants stimulated important though gradual changes in the socio-economic relations existing in the Russian zone. It gave rise to a process of modernization on both peasant farms and great landed estates. The rural population began to sell its produce on an increasing scale, and became an increasingly important consumer of industrial goods. Part of the rural population moved to towns, some obtaining employment in industry which had begun to develop. Production increased. Gradually, the Kingdom of Poland, its Western part in particular, was becoming the most modern and economically advanced area in the whole of the Russian Empire.

These important changes took place under conditions of extremely severe repression imposed on the Russian zone following the suppression of the Insurrection. The state of emergency decreed during the Insurrection, was maintained as a permanent feature after its suppression. Many death sentences were passed, and tens of thousands were sentenced to forced labour in Siberia, thousands of families were deported to eastern provinces of the Empire. Over three thousand estates belonging to members of the gentry who had fought in the Insurrection were confiscated. Repressive measures were also applied against the Catholic Church, priests were deported and monasteries closed down. The Greek-Catholic Uniate Church which was dominant in the Eastern part of the Kingdom of Poland, was suppressed and its members forcibly "converted" to the Russian Orthodox faith. The fierce resistance put up by the persecuted members of the Uniate Church resounded throughout Europe. At the same time differences distinguishing the legal-political system in the Kingdom of Poland from the rest of the Russian Empire were systematically eliminated. Within a few years, all central offices in the Kingdom were abolished, and the organizational structure of local authorities was changed and subordinated to St. Petersburg. Russification of the Kingdom of Poland continued parallel with the systematic elimination of its separate identity which had been guaranteed by the Congress of Vienna. Polish teachers, officials and judges were dismissed and replaced by Russians. Use of the Polish language was banned in every sphere of life. This was a particularly severe blow to the education system. Russian authorities destroyed every possibility of an autonomous functioning of Polish society; social, cultural and educational institutions were closed down. The printed word was subject to extremely severe censorship. In consequence, political life in the Russian zone came to a standstill.

A marked fall of interest in the Polish cause at that time in Europe had a disheartening influence on Polish society. For France, after her defeat in the war with Prussia and the creation of the German Empire, the primary problem had become the search for security against her powerful neighbour across the Rhine. These efforts gave birth to the unnatural — as it might appear — alliance between the democratic, bourgeois Third Republic and the despotically ruled Russia. This alliance maintained Russian rule in Poland and also meant acceptance of the *status quo* of the other two partitioning states.

The Kingdom of Prussia, the second partitioning power, though transformed into a constitutional monarchy in the mid-19th century, following its international successes (Germany was reunited under Prussian dominance in 1871), intensified its anti-Polish policy. Conducted by other methods than those practised by Imperial Russia, this policy aimed at Germanization of Poles who had become Prussian subjects as a result of the partitions. During the *Kulturkampf* (cultural struggle) period of Bismarck's government, the persecution of Poles gained in intensity and also extended to the Catholic Church, to which the vast majority of Poles belonged. Germanization was conducted in schools, offices, and the army; Polish localities were given German names, efforts were even made to Germanize Polish christian and family names. A large number of Poles were expelled from the country under various pretexts. In the 20th century, laws on the forced expropriation of Polish peasants were passed.

Whereas Russian and Prussian policies, aimed respectively at Russification and Germanization of the Polish population, differed only in their methods of operation, the situation in the Austrian zone changed radically towards the end of the 1860s. Weakened by military defeats, the Habsburg Empire became a constitutional monarchy, and the nations which formed part of it were granted a degree of autonomy and certain freedoms. Galicia was granted autonomy and its own Parliament which assembled in Lvov, the capital of the province, together with various institutions of local government subordinate to this Parliament. The administration, jurisdiction and education system were completely re-polonized. Galicia was the only partition zone where Polish universities were allowed to exist, in Cracow and Lvov, as well as a network of Polish primary and secondary schools. Polish national culture, ruthlessly persecuted in the other partition zones, was allowed to develop without any major restrictions. Cracow and Lvov became active centres of culture, radiating an influence over all former Polish territories. Within this autonomy, the conservatively-minded local gentry gained decisive influence and its selfish social policy met with determined resistance on the part of progressive forces.

The Birth of Modern Political Movements

When, after 1864, virtually all forms of national activity were banned in the Russian zone, the lively ideological and intellectual movement known as positivism, which embraced educated circles in the 1870s, gained in significance. Positivism was inspired by the development of the exact and also the social sciences and by the birth of the modern science of sociology; it glorified freedom of scientific research and the development of human thought, it spread the cult of education, urged people to work for the good of society, and proclaimed the capitalist transformation of social relations. Positivism played a large role in modernizing the way of thinking of relatively broad sections of society. The leading representatives of this ideology were Aleksander Świętochowski, Bolesław Prus and Adolf Dygasiński.

The number of workers increased as capitalism developed in the Kingdom of Poland. They lived in extremely harsh conditions and were, moreover, persecuted by tsarist officials on account of their nationality. Russia, known at that time as the "prison of nations", had no labour legislation of the kind emerging in other European countries. It was forbidden to form associations or to strike. Thus, it was not surprising that it was among the workers that a movement was born with the aim of overthrowing the tsarist régime, destroying existing social relations and winning national freedoms.

In 1864 the First International, which had just been founded that year, voiced its solidarity with the insurgents who fought against the tsarist régime. Many Poles were influenced by the thought of Marx and Engels. The latter recognized Polish aspirations for independence not only as just and valid but also worthy of support since they could lead to the overthrowing of the partitioning powers who were the pillars of absolutism and reaction in Europe.

Lenin, the founder of the Bolshevik Party, later took up these ideas and applied them to the new conditions. Polish emigrés joined the International, and at least several hundered took part in the Paris Commune. One of the participants was General Jarosław Dąbrowski, co-organizer of the January Insurrection and commander of the Commune's armed forces.

Polish emigré links with socialism developed through organizations in Western Europe, especially in Switzerland, and also illegal Marxist circles in Russia. The International Social Revolutionary Proletariat Party was established in Warsaw in 1882. One of its founders was a young socialist leader, Ludwik Waryński. Working under the most difficult conditions, this party formed an organization of several hundred workers, published its own newspapers and pamphlets. However, the authorities were on their track; arrests were made and harsh sentences were passed; twenty-two years after the execution of members of the National Government of the January Insurrection on the slopes of Warsaw's Citadel, four members of the Proletariat were hanged there. From this moment onwards, despite constant repression on the part of the Russian authorities, and the unwilling, sometimes even hostile, attitude of the Polish property-owning classes, the Polish workers' movement continued to extend its influence.

In 1892 the Polish Socialist Party (PPS) was founded and recognized the struggle for Polish independence as a necessary precondition for the realization of social changes. This party, which was not a homogeneous body, found itself under the influence of social democratic thought in Western Europe. One of its leading ideologists was Bolesław Limanowski. Marxist thought was developed by Kazimierz Kelles-Krauz. Among the PPS leaders, Józef Piłsudski played an important role.

Some of its leaders considered the programme of the party to be a contravention of socialist principles. They put forward as an ultimate aim the construction of a socialist system, which was to arise as a result of the international revolution, following the victory of which the national question would solve itself spontaneously. In 1893 those who held this view founded the Social Democracy of the Kingdom of Poland (from 1900 the Social Democracy of the Kingdom of Poland and Lithuania — SDKPiL) whose active leaders included Feliks Dzierżyński, Julian Marchlewski and Rosa Luxemburg, who later collaborated with the Bolsheviks. Socialist parties, similar to the Polish Socialist Party, were also formed in the other partition zones. Ignacy Daszyński, one of the leading figures of the socialist movement, was to become an eminent politician and parliamentarian in the ranks of the Polish Social Democratic Party of Galicia and Cieszyn Silesia.

Other contemporary Polish political parties were also organized towards the end of the century. The main legal branch of the secret National League, which was involved in insurrectionist conspiracies, was the National Democratic Party or National Democracy, whose leader was Roman Dmowski. The National Democracy conducted activities to arouse national awareness, particularly among the peasants, and organized clandestine education. Gradually, however, this party became a distinctly conservative group with a more and more pronounced nationalist image.

The Polish Peasant Party was formed in 1895, in the Austrian zone, during the political struggles for the democratization of existing political institutions. The peasant movement aimed at patriotic work among the peasants, a voice in national affairs and, in the future, the recovery of Polish independence. One of the most prominent leaders of this movement was Wincenty

Witos, who was later to receive the highest state dignities in independent Poland, but always remained a peasant at heart. The constitutional nature of government in the Austrian and Prussian zones enabled Polish politicians in those provinces to conduct legal activity. In consequence, Galicia in particular became a base for the activity of political forces in the Russian zone, where Polish groups could only act underground, in an atmosphere of continued repression, inseparable from the despotic methods of government. Before the First World War, Lenin also took advantage of the situation in Galicia and directed the Russian revolutionary movement from there.

In the Prussian zone, the policy of ruthless Germanization and the deportation of Poles led to unity among the Polish population in the face of the common threat. Various socio-economic and cultural initiatives were undertaken under the positivist slogans of "organic work" and "work at the roots". A whole network of Polish socio-economic organizations was formed, agricultural circles, peasant banks, as well as choral societies and theatrical groups. These organizations provided a defence against measures applied by the Prussian administration and successfully went against Germanization. Poles joined in this bloodless struggle in ever increasing numbers, a struggle in which the Catholic Church played a role of great importance. With the awakening of national awareness among the peasant masses of the Poznań region, Pomerania and among workers of Silesia, one of the most industrialized regions of Europe, the influence of the National Democracy was gradually increasing. Among the many political leaders, Wojciech Korfanty, a young politician from Silesia, who was connected with the National Democracy, distinguished himself by his political activities in the Reichstag.

The evolution of modern national ties was influenced by many factors. Among them was an awareness of national traditions, the Catholic religion common to virtually all Poles and the rites of the Catholic Church. In the Russian zone, the Church was the only large Polish institution whose influence radiated over virtually the whole society. National culture played a role of tremendous, steadily growing importance. Despite nonexistence of a Polish state, despite the severe restrictions imposed in the Russian and Prussian zones, a specific kind of social and private patronage evolved in occupied Polish territories, replacing activities conducted elsewhere by the state.

Foundations and private organizations were established on Polish territory, which encouraged intellectual life in all its various forms. The name of Poland was kept alive by scholars of world renown such as Maria Skłodowska-Curie, Ignacy Domeyko and Edmund Strzelecki; by Nobel-prize winning writers such as Henryk Sienkiewicz, author of the *Trilogy* and *Quo Vadis?*, which was translated into many languages, and Władysław Reymont, author of the tetralogy *The Peasants*; by painters and musicians, the most famous of whom was the celebrated pianist and composer, Ignacy Jan Paderewski. The visual arts and music flourished, and the composers of those years shaped the face of Polish national culture for decades to come.

Polish Society During the Revolutionary Period 1905—07

The Russo-Japanese war and the outbreak of the Russian revolution in the years 1905—07 resounded loudly throughout Polish territories. The Kingdom of Poland became the scene of large demonstrations and strikes. In June 1905, workers in Łódź staged an abortive attempt at a rising against Tsarist Russia. Membership of workers' groups conducting semilegal activities multiplied, each of them numbering several thousand members. Trade unions with mass membership arose. Alongside the proletariat, Polish intellectuals developed equally energetic activity. A network of educational organizations, civic institutions, centres of artistic and cultural activity, which sprang up almost overnight, was due primarily to the efforts of the intelligentsia. The press, and publications in general, also showed a notable development. A factor of extreme importance was the political development of the rural population. The movement for restoring the use of the Polish language in local administrative organs and communal offices, initiated by the peasants, was a vital expression of their patriotism. The general boycott of Russian schools became a powerful national manifestation of patriotism. The tsarist régime was forced to make concessions: the Kingdom of Poland gained the right to send its representatives to the Russian State Duma (the Russian Parliament first constituted in 1906 — translator's note), administrative pressure was eased, language rights were broadened, cultural activities were permitted.

Those revolutionary years were not only a period of large-scale political activity among the broadest sections of society, but also a period when polarization became manifest. Strikes entailed conflicts of an unprecedented scale between the proletariat on the one hand, and the bourgeoisie and owners of great estates on the other. The latter had recourse repeatedly to the assistance of the administration and military. As the leading political representative of the Polish property-owning classes, the National Democracy joined in the struggle against the socialist movement. This clear division between the right wing, led by the National Democracy, and the left wing, by no means united at the time, continued through four decades.

In those revolutionary years, conflicts within the Polish Socialist Party grew in strength. Piłsudski and his followers regarded the Revolution as the beginning of a new insurrection. Under their leadership, the Party's Combat Organization carried out many assassination attempts against the most hated government functionaries and undertook guerrilla operations. The Russian authorities responded with repression. Many members of the Combat Organization were killed in action, or apprehended and hanged. Revolutionary activities widened the gap between the Party's right and left. As a result of ideological and tactical differences a rift occurred within the Polish Socialist Party. Piłsudski's followers formed the Revolutionary Faction of the Polish Socialist Party and the leftists founded the Left Wing of the Polish Socialist Party which, on many questions, adopted an attitude similar to that of the SDKPiL.

Despite measures taken by tsarist authorities, aimed at restricting earlier concessions, the period which followed the 1905—07 revolution facilitated diversified cultural and educational activity. Nonetheless, the reprisals against working-class leaders caused a marked reduction in the activity of proletarian parties in the Russian zone.

In the meantime, military preparations anticipating an armed conflict between the partitioning powers were undertaken in Galicia. The clandestine Active Combat Union, founded in 1908, with Józef Piłsudski as its Commandant, formed the legal military training organization known as the Rifle Union. Political support for the Active Combat Union came from the Revolutionary Faction of the Polish Socialist Party and progressive circles of the Galician intelligentsia. In view of the fact that the military movement was steadily gaining increasing popularity, among young people in particular, military training organizations also sprang up in those environments which had little in common with ideals of armed struggle for independence.

The emergence of two opposed military blocs (with Russia in one and the other two partitioning powers in the other) contributed to the birth of two opposed political orientations in Polish society. One, subsequently known as activist, had the liberation of the Russian zone as its primary aim, followed by its eventual incorporation with Galicia to form a state which would constitute a separate distinct part of the Habsburg monarchy. The other orientation, known as passive, aimed at the unification of all Polish lands under the rule of the Russian tsar. The National Democracy stood at the head of the latter.

Poland in the First World War (1914—18)

The outbreak of the First World War awakened Polish hopes. It seemed certain that war between the partitioning powers would bring fulfilment of the hopes and efforts of the Polish nation, which, deprived of independence, divided and subjected to intense Russification and Germanization, had managed to preserve its national identity. These hopes, however, were not to be fulfilled until much later. The belligerent powers kept silence on the Polish question. Only the Russian commander-in-chief came out with vague promises. Though these promises were not kept as long as the tsarist régime lasted, the very fact they were made strengthened the position of the pro-Russian political camp in Poland.

On the other side of the front, Józef Piłsudski's efforts to start, with the support of partisan detachments, an insurrection against Russia did not prove fruitful. Piłsudski's original unit became the nucleus of the Polish Legions, an auxiliary force fighting on the side of the Austrian army. For the first time since the collapse of the November Insurrection regular Polish soldiers took up arms against the tsar. It was the misfortune of the divided nation that it had to fight with all partitioning powers at the same time. For a short while, a similar unit operated on the Russian side of the front. In 1915, German and Austro-Hungarian armies occupied the Russian zone. The prolonged war and consequent lack of reserves caused the

Central Powers to issue a declaration in November 1916, concerning the creation of a Kingdom of Poland dependent on themselves. They also set up organs of the future state, first the Provisional Council of State, and later, the Regency Council. However, their hopes of thus securing volunteers for a new army were disappointed. Moreover, the imperialist plans of the new rulers became increasingly evident. The fulfilment of certain demands (the language question, Polish schooling, a limitation of the system of anti-Polish reprisals applied by Russian authorities right up to the end of Russian rule over those territories), did not stand in the way of their systematic looting of the country, which they stripped of food and raw materials and ruined its industry. Their ruthless methods and deportation of thousands of Poles to do forced labour provoked increasing resistance.

Meanwhile, the Polish question acquired international dimensions. At the beginning of 1917, President Woodrow Wilson of the United States advocated the Polish nation's right to statehood. The overthrow of the tsarist régime had an enormous significance. The Russian workers' movement proclaimed Poland's right to independence in the Petrograd Soviet of the Workers' Deputies. So did the Russian government headed by Prince Lvov, but his concessions were hedged with important qualifications. After Russia, the first voice in Europe on the Polish question was raised in the Italian Parliament. Developments in Russia brought about a change in the attitude of those groups in Poland which formerly had been prepared to collaborate with the Central Powers against the tsarist régime. The Revolutionary Faction of the Polish Socialist Party and the "Liberation" Polish Peasant Party undertook underground activities against the occupying powers. Piłsudski dissolved the Polish Legions and many of their members (the Legions totalled some 30,000 men), who refused to cooperate further with the Central Powers were interned. Piłsudski himself was imprisoned by the Germans, together with his closest collaborator Kazimierz Sosnkowski. The semi-legal Polish Military Organization, headed by Piłsudski's followers, went underground and started action against the Germans and Austrians. In the summer of 1917, supporters of "passivism", relying on the Western Powers, formed a National Committee in Paris. The Coalition Powers recognized this Committee as an official Polish organization exercising political control over the newly-established Polish army in France. Roman Dmowski stood at the head of the Committee. In the final stage of the war, seven well-trained and equipped Polish divisions, commanded by General Józef Haller, fought the Germans on the Western front.

The overthrow of the bourgeois. Russian Provisional Government and the establishment of Soviet authority significantly influenced the future of the Polish cause. The party which gained control proclaimed the slogan of national self-determination, which had been formulated by Lenin in 1903; it recognized without reservation Poland's right to independence and gave expression to this attitude in its practical moves and legal documents (The Declaration of Rights of the Peoples of Russia, The Decree on Peace, etc.). At the same time, the socialist revolution freed the coalition powers, France in particular, from their obligations towards former Russian governments. A series of statements on the Polish question ensued; the most famous was President Wilson's message (Point 13 of this message defined one of the peace aims of the coalition to be the restoration of an independent Polish state with a free access to the sea). For France, which lost Russia as a former anti-German ally, the restoration of an independent Poland became a necessity. The real imperialist aspirations of the Central Powers in Eastern Europe became evident after the downfall of the Kerensky régime. They found clear expression in the treaty of Brest Litovsk signed in February 1918 by the Central Powers with their dependent state of the Ukraine, by which they handed over to the latter part of the Kingdom of Poland, a move which provoked massive resistance on the part of Polish society. A wave of strikes and demonstrations engulfed the country, officials handed in their resignations en masse. Sabotage became rampant. The number of supporters of cooperation with the Central Powers quickly declined. Even the Regency Council, the nucleus of supreme authority in the Kingdom of Poland dependent on those Powers, manifested its determination to break with them and establish its autonomy.

Independence Regained

The defeat of the Central Powers came in the autumn of 1918. The Austrian partition zone fell into Polish hands. German and Austrian troops were disarmed and expelled from the southern part of the Kingdom of Poland. Socialists and members of the Peasant Party, together with Piłsudski's followers, formed a Provisional People's Government of the Polish Republic in Lublin on 6/7 November. Ignacy Daszyński became Prime Minister and General Edward Śmigły-Rydz, who was Piłsudski's subordinate in the Legions and commander of the Polish Military Organization after Piłsudski's arrest, was elected Minister of War. The Provisional People's Government, the first independent government in the revived state, proclaimed Poland a parliamentary republic, and promised an armed struggle for the liberation of Polish territory still under German occupation. A few days after this government was formed, the Germans were expelled from Warsaw and the rest of the former Kingdom of Poland, partly by force of arms. Warsaw became the new seat of government of the independent state and Józef Piłsudski, released from a German prison, became provisional leader of the state. The liberated territories were surrounded by more than a million German soldiers, who still remained a powerful military force in Eastern Europe. Thus the liberation of Poland's western territories also came about as a result of fighting. At the end of December 1918 an insurrection broke out in Poznań. After several weeks of fighting conducted by improvised units which soon numbered several thousand soldiers, a considerable part of the former Prussian zone was liberated.

For the Polish nation the restoration of independence was a momentous event. Liberation, establishment of its own state, is always a tremendous success for a conquered nation, particularly so to a nation with a millenary history of independent statehood, a nation which had never reconciled itself to the loss of independence. Divided between the three partitioning powers, the Polish nation preserved its sense of identity. During the over 120 years of subjugation it repeatedly demonstrated its will to win back independence in armed risings. The period of subjugation was over and it became possible to tackle the disastrous legacy of foreign rule and to return to normal existence and unhindered development.

Poland was reborn as a democratic state — a republic which proclaimed political freedoms guaranteeing the masses influence on the country's government. At the same time, it was a capitalist state in which, despite the promise of various social reforms, the decisive role was retained by the property-owning classes. The latter's selfish attitude intensified tensions and social conflicts. Strikes, often brutally suppressed by the authorities, broke out in factories and on large landed estates. The working masses had to gain their rights by struggle. The revolutionary upheavals in Europe facilitated their aims. The bourgeois attitude was influenced by fear of socialism which had already been established successfully in Soviet Russia. This fear resulted in the acceptance of democratic-republican state institutions in Poland by reactionary political forces and at the same time helped left-wing groups to attain their aims.

In January 1919, as a result of an understanding between the Polish politicians at home and in Paris, Piłsudski appointed a new Cabinet, led by Ignacy Paderewski, widely known not only as a virtuoso and composer, but also as an advocate of the Polish cause in the allied countries. This government held elections to the Constituent Assembly — the Legislative Seym. The majority of votes was gained by the Right — the National Democrats and their allies. Peasant organizations also played an important role in the Seym, although no lasting cooperation was achieved between them. The Parliamentary Left Wing was weak. Radical peasant party members and socialists gained 20 per cent of the seats, however the revolutionary left-wing was not represented at all.

On 16 December 1918, the Social Democratic Party of the Kingdom of Poland and Lithuania and the Left Wing of the Polish Socialist Party joined to form the Communist Workers' Party of Poland, from 1925 onwards known as the Communist Party of Poland. This party, which believed that Europe, Poland included, was on the verge of a socialist revolution, stood in sharp opposition to the state, viewing it one-sidedly merely as an organ of the rule of the property-owning classes. Propagating the formation of councils of workers' and peasants' deputies, regarded as an instrument in the struggle for the victory of socialism, it opposed elections to the Seym. Persecuted by the authorities and right-wing forces, and subsequently outlawed, the Communist Party of Poland was forced to work under-ground. Shortly afterwards, the councils of workers' deputies, formed in a number of centres, were liquidated by the authorities.

Unable to act publicly, hounded by the authorities, and imprisoned for years at a stretch, Polish communists fought uncompromisingly for the fundamental interests of the masses. They organized strikes and demonstrations under the most difficult conditions. In increasingly wider circles they propagated socialist class consciousness, spread word of the victorious socialist revolution and showed the need for closer relations with the Soviet state.

The Struggle over the Polish Frontiers

At the Peace Congress which met in Paris at the beginning of 1919, Poland was represented by Paderewski and Dmowski. Despite support from France, Poland's demands were only partially taken into account in the Versailles Peace Treaty. Apart from the liberated Great Poland, the stretch of land near the Baltic, tendentiously referred to in German propaganda a "Corridor", was also restored to Poland. Gdańsk, the ancient Polish port, was declared a Free City, connected with its Polish hinterland by a complicated and ambiguous system of obligations. The future of former East and West Prussia, as well as Silesia, was to be decided by a plebiscite. For the time being, the German administration remained operative there, which placed the Polish side in a worse situation.

The Polish population in Silesia refused to submit to these decisions. Determined that Silesia should be incorporated with Poland, they took up a struggle against the German pressure and proceeded to organize self-defence organizations. In August 1919 an uprising broke out in response to German terror. After its suppression, the Silesians did not abandon further attempts to join Poland. Their military organization remained in existence, preparations for self-defence continued. In August 1920, German chauvinists launched an attack on the Polish population and Allied detachments which had been dispatched to Silesia to supervise the plebiscite. This gave rise to the second Silesian Uprising, which brought about an improvement in the situation of the Polish population. The plebiscite, which was held in Silesia in March 1921, only partially reflected actual national proportions in this area. Poland received 479,000 votes and Germany 706,000. This result was influenced by the votes of 200,000 people who were born in Silesia but lived in the Reich and who were brought over to Silesia solely for the purpose of casting their votes in the plebiscite. At the news of a plan to hand over the greater part of the plebiscite areas to Germany, a third Silesian Uprising broke out on 2/3 May 1921. The insurgents, led by Wojciech Korfanty, soon occupied territory as far as the Odra River. Despite their comparative lack of arms (having signed the Treaty of Versailles, the Polish government did not want to run the risk of being accused of violating it and avoided giving them open aid), the insurgents' improvised detachments kept their hold on the recovered territory and put up strong resistance to an enemy who was superior in numbers and equipment. The battles in defence of St. Anne's Hill have gone down in history. On 5 July 1921, on the initiative of the Inter-Allied Commission a truce was signed. The future of Silesia was ultimately to be decided by an international conference.

The Silesian uprisings were without precedent. Three times in as many years, Silesian workers and peasants rose in armed rebellion against the overwhelming forces of the enemy. The uprisings gained increasing military successes; in each successive attempt the number of insurgents increased and as many as 60,000 people fought in the third uprising. This constituted clear proof that the population of Silesia, which had been separated from Poland for a period of several centuries, desired to become part of the new independent Polish state. The Coalition had to take this into account. In October 1921 the League of Nations granted Poland part of the plebiscite territory inhabited by one million people and containing the majority of the Silesian industrial enterprises. In June 1922, part of Upper Silesia, which was regained by Poland, was placed under Polish administration.

Restored to independence after well over a century of foreign domination, Poland did not have fixed frontiers, as a result of which conflicts flared up with practically all her neighbours.

There were disputes with Czechoslovakia over Cieszyn Silesia, which was mainly inhabited by Poles, but constituted an area of great economic importance to Czechoslovakia. This conflict was solved as a result of the mediation of the Coalition Powers, but a large number of Poles still remained outside Poland. The situation on the Polish-German border was similar. The disputed territories were divided in such a way that — according to German statistics — more than a million Poles lived inside Germany.

The most serious conflict, however, was with Poland's eastern neighbours. Even during the aboliton of Austrian rule in Galicia, fighting between Poland and Ukrainian nationalists broke out over Eastern Galicia, which was an area of constant dispute. The conflict began with the Ukrainians seizing Lvov. The local Polish population resisted. Regular fighting between Polish and Ukrainian troops continued till the summer of 1919 and ended with the Ukrainians being forced back across the Zbruch River. A territory inhabited mainly by Ukrainians, with the exception of towns, came under Polish rule. The Ukrainians remained unreconciled to Polish rule throughout the entire period of the Second Commonwealth. At the same time the generally anti-Ukrainian policies of the Polish government led to acute conflicts between the two peoples.

The regions to the east of the territory of the former Kingdom of Poland became an area of conflict as well. Occupying German troops began their withdrawal from these territories in the spring of 1919. In their place local centres of power sprang up and Soviet rule was gradually established.

From the moment independence was regained, the Polish government pursued anti-Soviet policies in line with the interventional moves of the Allied Powers. Despite the fact that the Soviet government proposed establishing diplomatic relations, in February 1919 Poland launched a military campaign. By the end of the year, Polish forces, whose commander-in-chief was Józef Piłsudski, occupied territories up to the river Dvina in the North and the river Zbruch in the South. Piłsudski wanted to detach the Ukraine and Byelorussia from Soviet Russia and annex them to Poland in some kind of federation. For this reason he rejected Soviet peace overtures. Soviet Russia, which was involved in heavy fighting with the white counter-revolutionary armies supported by the Allied Powers, was anxious to conclude peace with Poland, even at the price of far-reaching territorial concessions. Lenin considered that territorial concessions in Poland's favour would constitute a proper way of ending the age-old quarrel between the Polish and Russian peoples, a quarrel in which Poland had suffered so much at the hands of the tsarist régime. Piłsudski rejected these proposals, however, and concluded an agreement with Hetman Petlura, commander of the Ukrainian separatists, and together with him launched a large offensive. In May 1920, Polish troops under General Śmigły-Rydz captured Kiev. Thus, for Soviet Russia the war with Poland became the most important military problem of the time. A month later, the Soviet army began a counter-offensive and in August 1920 reached the outskirts of Warsaw. A Polish manoeuvre in the Warsaw region once again changed the military position. The Polish army launched a successful offensive and the front shifted far to the East.

In the meantime, negotiations continued and bore fruit in the signing of a peace treaty in Riga in March 1921. Poland's frontiers with Soviet Russia were demarcated to the East of the Curzon line, based on ethnic considerations, which had already been provisionally established in December 1919 by the Allied Powers. This meant that Poland received areas inhabited mostly by Byelorussians and Ukrainians. Disputes continued with Lithuania over Lithuania's historical capital of Vilna, which in the summer of 1920 found itself in Lithuanian hands but was captured by Polish forces in the autumn. Attempts to settle the conflict (also undertaken in the League of Nations) proved unsuccessful and a state of sharp tension between the two states continued almost up to the outbreak of the Second World War.

The Social and Economic Structure of the Second Commonwealth

Poland's land area at this time was 388,600 sq. km. and its population rose from 27.2 million inhabitants in 1921 to over 35 million in 1939. About two thirds of these were ethnically Polish. Ukrainians were the largest minority and made up about 15 per cent of the population, and were followed by Jews, Byelorussians, and, lastly, Germans. Ten million Poles lived outside the country. The largest Polish communities existed in areas around the borders with Germany, the Soviet Union and Czechoslovakia. Several million Poles were living in the United States.

Poland's population was predominantly engaged in agriculture — more than two thirds of the total. Small peasant farms of an area up to five hectares, not big enough to assure their owners sufficient means of livelihood, predominated, particularly in the former Austrian zone. Almost half of the land and forests was in the hands of great landowners or the state, and land hunger constituted a serious social and political problem for the peasants. The owners of private estates, descended in general from the Polish gentry, wielded sufficient influence to effectively oppose the realization of radical agrarian reforms. Many people in rural districts were unemployed and short of the essential means of making a livelihood.

Two statutes on land reform were passed, but the distribution of land took a long time. Over the 20-year period landlords' holdings decreased by only 3 million hectares, or 50 per cent of all the arable land in their possession. This could not essentially improve the position of the rural population, whose low purchasing power held back the nation's economic development. In 1921 only 24 per cent of the entire population lived in cities, although immediately before the Second World War this percentage rose to nearly 30 per cent. Industry (mining, textile and food industry were comparatively well developed) was located mainly in southeast and central Poland (Silesia, Dąbrowa Basin, Cracow, Warsaw and Łódź regions). Small workshops, often using artisan methods of production, predominated. Nearly half of the labour force worked in small enterprises employing no more than five workers.

Poland emerged from the First World War devastated. Ninety per cent of the country had been affected by military operations, some areas over long periods of time. Losses were estimated at two thousand million dollars. Nonetheless war destruction was made good within a short period of time. The question of rebuilding and starting up industry posed far greater difficulties. Immediately after the war industrial output was only half the pre-war level. It was not until the economic boom of 1928—29 that the level of production increased considerably. Many new industrial establishments were built at this time, but at the beginning of the 1930s, Poland, together with the whole capitalist world, suffered from an economic crisis of unprecedented magnitude. Compared with the previous period, production fell by almost 50 per cent and unemployment rose sharply. The standard of living among the peasants also deteriorated. In the mid-1930s the economy began to revive and production and employment gradually increased; the economy was entering a flourishing period. Taking the output in 1928 as 100, the figure for 1938 was 119. Serious unemployement, however, still persisted, accounting for 10 per cent of the labour force.

For many reasons the Polish economy did not develop uniformly. The capitalist economic cycle of booms followed by stagnation and serious crises, was made worse by Poland's lack of financial resources. Many branches of the economy were heavily dependent on foreign investors whose approach was more or less neocolonialist. Attempts at overcoming this dependence produced no substantial results. Certain branches of industry were non-existent in Poland and part of its production was not adapted to the country's needs. From the years of partition she inherited a weakly developed rail and road network and poorly regulated rivers. Efforts to change this state of affairs continued throughout the inter-war period. Though complete success was not attained, the three different partition zones were integrated into a single uniform economic organism. Great progress was made in the building of railways. A number of lines were built linking the country's most important centres. The punctuality of the Polish railways was proverbial, and their standard, as well as the quality of service, was high. The largest and most modern port was established on the Baltic in Gdynia, a small fishing village that was transformed into a city with 100,000 inhabitants. A small but modern merchant marine and navy were built. In 1936, the so-called Central Industrial District, an unusually daring and large-scale industrial complex, was built in the most backward and overpopulated areas of Central Poland. It included above all heavy industry and armament factories. One of the principal authors of the Central Industrial District project was Eugeniusz Kwiatkowski, for many years a Minister and Vice-Premier, who exercised a great influence on the nation's economic development. The outbreak of the Second World War prevented the completion of this undertaking.

Warsaw also became a great centre of modern industry. The city itself was modernized and developed rapidly. In this respect great services were rendered by Stefan Starzyński, the last pre-war Mayor of the Polish capital. Work on development and modernization also proceeded rapidly in other large cities, such as Poznań, Cracow and Lvov.

In the inter-war period Poland made great economic strides forward. Many industrial establishments in the chemical, electrical engineering and metal industry were modernized and many new ones built. Work began on the Polish armaments and transport industries. Goods manufactured by many branches of Polish industry were up to the highest standards in the world. The existence of Poland as a state facilitated the process of integrating the Polish lands. Together with the formation of a uniform economic organism, the unification of the judicial system and socio-political institutions made progress. This provided the essential conditions for eliminating parochial attitudes which were the aftermath of the partitions, and forming close national ties. The restoration of independence had particularly great significance for the development of national culture. A Polish educational system — starting with elementary schools and going all the way up to universities and the most learned institutions — was established and developed. Illiteracy — a grim legacy of partition — considerably declined. The fact that Poland again existed as a state had an invigorating effect on the development of literature, science and the fine arts. While in the first decade of independence, the most prominent role was played by writers from the past epoch — Stefan Żeromski, Władysław Reymont and Andrzej Strug — the final years before the Second World War saw an upsurge of new talent represented by revolutionary writers like Bruno Jasieński and Leon Kruczkowski, socially concerned writers like Maria Dąbrowska and Zofia Nałkowska, and such precursors of new currents in literature as Bruno Schulz, Witold Gombrowicz and — older than the previous two — Stanisław Ignacy Witkiewicz. As regards poetry, suffice it here to mention the names of Jan Kasprowicz, Leopold Staff, Julian Tuwim, Jan Lechoń, Antoni Słonimski, Julian Przyboś and Władysław Broniewski. A new phenomenon arose in the shape of cultural activity aimed at the widest possible public. Thus, besides the works of Karol Szymanowski, and the piano and violin contests named after Frédéric Chopin and Henryk Wieniawski, appreciated by the élite, there was also the career of the famous tenor Jan Kiepura, who enjoyed the popularity of a star. The cult that grew up around his person also testifies to the role played by the mass media in the dissemination of culture. Cinema became a universal form of entertainment, especially in the towns. An increasingly important role was played by radio. Shortly before the war nearly a million families possessed a radio set. The Warsaw radio transmitter, put into operation in 1931, was the most powerful in the world.

✻

Despite the factors hampering Poland's development — such as the social structure and the backwardness inherited from the partition period — the cultural level of the nation as a whole gradually rose as did the level of self-awareness. The generation that lived through the period of the Second Commonwealth passed its severest test in the years of occupation during the Second World War.

Poland During the Period of Parliamentary Government

On 17 March 1921, after a long and protracted debate, the Seym approved the so-called March Constitution based on institutions of the Third Republic in France. This Constitution introduced a parliamentary system of government and the Seym and the Senate, formed for a 5-year term after democratic elections, were vested with legislative powers. The Seym was the chief governing body, and the Council of Ministers was responsible to it. The role of the Senate, and that of the President, who was elected by both houses, was relatively limited. The Constitution proclaimed a broad range of citizens' rights and liberties, although in practice these were often infringed upon. This was a result of the alignment of class forces in Poland (it was difficult for the working classes to take advantage of rights whose implementation would mean a curtailment of the economic predominance of the property-owning classes), and also of the discrimination practised against national minorities, especially Ukrainian and Byelorussian peasants. The considerable restriction of civil rights and liberties made it impossible for the revolutionary movement to conduct its activities legally.

In 1922, elections were held to the Seym and the Senate and the Right received the majority of votes, followed by national minorities acting together. Contrary to the desires of the Right, Gabriel Narutowicz, an eminent expert in hydroelectric engineering, was elected president. The National Democracy unleashed an unusually vitriolic campaign against the President, who was assassinated a few days after the election. The acting head of state, Maciej Rataj, the well-known peasant leader and Marshal (Speaker) of the Seym, appointed an extraparliamentary cabinet with General Władysław Sikorski as premier. The assassination of President Narutowicz delayed the formation of a coalition between the National Democracy and the Piast Polish Peasant Party, the germs of which had come into existence immediately after the elections. This coalition came about in May 1923. The cabinet was headed, for the second time, by Wincenty Witos. This cabinet operated during the period of hyper-inflation which disorganized the economic life of the country. As a result of the unwillingness of right-wing groups to place financial burdens on the propertied classes, it was impossible to prevent the steady drop of the currency and the corresponding fall in the real value of wages. The country was shaken by mass strikes in which 848,000 workers took part in the course of one year, the largest number of strikers in the entire inter-war period. Tension in the Seym between the Left and the government grew. At the same time, the government was sharply criticized by Marshal Piłsudski who ostentatiously resigned from all his state offices. In November 1923, armed disturbances took place in Cracow. A workers' demonstration, which was banned by the authorities (a state of emergency was proclaimed) ended in fighting in the city. Dozens of people were killed. The government's position was undermined and it resigned. President Stanisław Wojciechowski appointed an extraparliamentary cabinet headed by an eminent economist, Professor Władysław Grabski, who undertook the introduction of financial reforms. He attained his purpose in the spring of 1924. The devalued Polish mark was replaced by the zloty, at a rate of 1 zł. = 1.8 million Polish marks. The zloty was a hard currency with a high rate of exchange of 5.18 zl. to the dollar.

The currency reform was Grabski's great success, especially as it had been carried through with the nation's own resources. Only later was success achieved in negotiating foreign loans, but on terms unfavourable to Poland. Poland's economic situation worsened at the beginning of 1925. Production and exports decreased and unemployment grew. An unfavourable factor was the violent severance of Polish-German trade relations, known as the customs war. Germany, until now Poland's main trading partner, attempted to subject Poland by economic pressure. The German plan failed, however it caused Poland serious economic difficulties.

The customs war was a sign of Germany's strengthened position in the international arena, proof of which were the Locarno Treaties (October 1925), which worsened Poland's international position. At the time, Poland's security was based primarily on the Franco-Polish Pact of 1921. Poland had aligned itself with France since regaining independence, but had now to face a

French tendency to neglect the alliance, a policy maintained by France for the next ten years. Attempts at a rapprochement with Czechoslovakia and the Soviet Union took place during the conference in Locarno; these, however, were moves made on the spur of the moment and not pursued by Polish diplomacy. The unfavourable international situation, economic difficulties and the lack of a definite majority in parliament, which made the formation of cabinets difficult, favoured the schemes of Marshal Piłsudski, who was once more preparing to assume power. His supporters in the army, who came from the former Legions, were involved in conspiracies. Marshal Piłsudski was supported by the Seym's Left Wing, who saw in him a barrier against rule by the National Democracy, which was suspected of preparing a coup d'état.

The May Coup d'État

Witos' third cabinet, based on a coaliton of the National Democracy and the Piast Party, was set up in May 1926, but met with hostile reception from the Left. Piłsudski took advantage of this situation and on 12 May marched on Warsaw at the head of troops loyal to him. Armed clashes broke out and 379 people lost their lives. After three days of fighting, Piłsudski and his followers, known as the *Sanacja* (moral rehabilitation) returned to power. The Seym lost its significance. After the resignation of the president the Seym chose Piłsudski's candidate, Professor Ignacy Mościcki, a prominent chemist, for this office. Parliament also voted a change of the Constitution, which seriously restricted the prerogatives of the Chambers.

The establishment of the new government coincided with a period of economic improvement, which was reflected in the country's internal relations. The Right was broken, the Left disorientated. This enabled the governing camp to broaden the ranks of its supporters. Gradually, new lines of division took shape. Some adherents of the National Democracy, among them great industrialists and landowners, gave their backing to the new government. New elections took place in March 1928. The Non-Party Bloc for Cooperation with the Government, an organization composed of numerous dissidents from other political parties and formed with the cooperation of the administration, participated in the elections. The civil service, from which opponents of the *Sanacja* had previously been removed, was active in the Bloc's election campaign and helped it to gain 30 per cent of the votes. After the elections, the Left and Centre opposition united to form the so-called "Centre-Left", which aimed at restoring parliamentary government and abolishing the *Sanacja* régime through concerted action in the Seym. The increasingly active opposition of the Centre-Left met with counter-measures from government circles. Both parliamentary Chambers were prematurely dissolved in August 1930 and the leaders of the opposition, headed by Witos, were illegally arrested, and imprisoned in the Fort of Brest. A dozen or so were found guilty and sentenced to several years imprisonment (up to three years). Some of the Brest prisoners emigrated before their sentences could be carried out. The Brest incident shocked public opinion and caused numerous protests from intellectuals, workers and peasant leaders. In the meantime the ruling camp took advantage of the events in order to strengthen its position. Elections held in the autumn of 1930 gained notoriety as a result of the wide-scale use of pressure on the electors and what were ironically referred to as "ballot box miracles". The *Sanacja* gained 46 per cent of the votes.

These events coincided with the beginning of the world-wide economic crisis. Unemployment rose sharply, and, as a result of the decline in agricultural prices, the countryside found itself in a severe plight. As well as the sit-ins and demonstrations by unemployed workers, the peasants too began to strike, their actions being coordinated by the Peasant Party (SL) which was formed in 1931 uniting the existing peasant parties and headed by Wincenty Witos. This party aimed at re-establishing a democratic government in Poland and introducing social, and above all agrarian, reforms. Witos, who lived abroad from 1933 onwards, was influential in the leadership of the SL which was led in his name by Maciej Rataj. The illegal Communist Party of Poland became reactivated and gained considerable successes, especially in leading demonstrations by the unemployed.

The beginning of the thirties saw a worsening of Polish-German relations. The Germans demanded a revision of the frontiers. At that time, after lengthy negotiations, a Polish-Soviet non-aggression pact was concluded. The direction of Polish foreign policy was taken over by Colonel Józef Beck. In 1934, the Pact was extended for ten years. Hitler's coming to power was greeted in Poland with anti-German military demonstrations and moves. In diplomatic circles it was rumoured that Piłsudski had proposed to France a joint preventive campaign against Hitler's Reich. Meanwhile, Great Britain, France and Italy strove to improve relations with the Nazi dictator. Negotiations were begun with a view to concluding a so-called Pact of Four between these four states, and so Poland too took steps to improve her relations with Germany. A non-aggression pact between the two countries was signed in January 1934.

From the beginning of the thirties, the government camp had been preparing changes in the Constitution. At the same time, it had introduced measures which restricted civic rights and toned down Labour Law regulations favourable to the workers. On 23 April 1935, a new Constitution, known as the April Constitution, was passed, by which the President became head of state, concentrating supreme and indivisible power and standing above all government bodies. Voting regulations, changed after the Constitution had been drafted, restricted the number of citizens with the right to vote, formed an "élite" which had the right to elect the Senate and prevented the opposition from declaring candidates for election. This Constitution was a definite step towards totalitarianism and reflected the consolidation of authoritarian methods of government. It met with opposition, especially on the part of the workers' movement, which had been shaken by Hitler's takeover in Germany. The Communist Party fought for an anti-fascist alliance to restore democracy in Poland, to block the way of fascism and for a popular front in defence of Poland's threatened independence. The trend towards a united front also grew within the Polish Socialist Party. In the elections to the Seym and Senate in the autumn of 1935, the anti-*Sanacja* forces organized a successful boycott by the majority of the electorate.

In May 1935 Józef Piłsudski died. The struggle for his political legacy divided the hitherto united ruling camp. Power resided ultimately in the hands of President Ignacy Mościcki and General (later Marshal) Edward Śmigły-Rydz who played an increasingly important political role. The so-called "group of colonels" (including Walery Sławek and Aleksander Prystor), who had headed the government since the beginning of the thirties, was removed from the government. Poland's last pre-war cabinet, headed by Premier General Sławoj-Składkowski, was formed in May 1936. The growth of right-wing tendencies in the ruling camp caused the defection of certain groups — especially among the intelligentsia — with liberal democratic leanings. Somewhat later, progressive circles among the intelligentsia, which up till now had been connected with the ruling party, formed Democratic Clubs. Numerous groups of white-collar workers became active in the Polish Socialist and Peasant Parties. The Communist Party of Poland extended its influence among the intelligentsia.

The years 1935—39 were characterized by mass strikes. In particular there developed the form of strike known as the Polish strike, where the workers occupied the factories. This type of strike was more than once countered with a sharp reaction from the authorities involving loss of life. A mass ten-day peasant strike, organized in August 1937 by the Peasant Party, produced a great response throughout the entire country. This was the most powerful political demonstration directed against the ruling camp before the Second World War. Its scope and the number of its participants (about one million people) made it the largest mass peasant demonstration in Europe. About 40 people were killed in clashes with the police. Despite their struggle with the dictatorial system at home, Poles remained faithful to their slogan, "For our freedom and yours". Thus when the civil war began in Spain in July 1936, several thousand Polish volunteers, organized chiefly by the Communist Party of Poland, fought on the Republican side.

The political spectrum in Poland during the years immediately preceding the Second World War was as follows: On the Right was the National Party, which represented a nationalistic, anti-parliamentary ideology, and sharply opposed not only the Left, but also the *Sanacja* ruling group, which they regarded as their main obstacle to power. A group comprising mainly politicians of the younger generation, broke away from the party in 1933 and formulated a distinctly fascist programme which attacked the National Party for yielding to the influence of parliamentarian and liberal concepts, especially on the part of the older leaders. This group organized the National Radical Camp (ONR) whose blatant nationalism and anti-Semitism was combined with anti-worker demonstrations and shrill anti-government demagogy. The National Radical Camp was dissolved by the government and continued semi-legal activities. The adherents of the *Sanacja* party grouped themselves into a National Unity Camp, formed in 1937. It sharply combatted both the Left and the National Democrats, who at the time were known as Nationalists. After the deaths of Piłsudski and Dmowski, young politicians, for whom former divisions were remote history, came to the fore, and the ideological gap between the erstwhile opponents began to close. The Communist Party of Poland, the Peasant Party and the Polish Socialist Party accused the *Sanacja* rulers and Nationalists of being anti-democratic and nationalistic, as well as of yielding to totalitarian influences. The Peasant Party and the Polish Socialist Party collaborated with one another and at the same time retained links with liberal circles in the ruling camp. The Peasant Party was a massive organization numbering about 200,000 members, while the Polish Socialist Party was less numerous (50,000 members) but its influence was multiplied by the so-called class trade unions which cooperated with it. After the Communist International had dissolved the Communist Party of Poland in 1938, communists in the country joined in the various campaigns undertaken by the Left. It should be noted that political groupings of the centre also became more active. A Party of Labour, representing a Christian Democratic point of view, was formed in 1937 under the auspices of Ignacy Paderewski, who at this time was living in Switzerland, and with the participation of General Sikorski, who sharply opposed the ruling camp (his dispute with Piłsudski dated from the time of the Legions). This grouping did not enjoy great influence.

During this period, Poland had an authoritarian system of government. The group that won power in May 1926, employed dictatorial methods (note should be taken of the fact that its composition had undergone a series of changes). The role of the Seym was seriously limited and only the supporters of the ruling camp participated in its work. Anti-democratic, even reactionary measures were introduced in internal policies. However, despite various harassments and oppression, a legal opposition did exist; independent newspapers were published despite censorship, and trade unions organized workers for strikes. The majority of organized workers were associated in trade unions independent of the *Sanacja*; almost half belonged to class unions which were socialist in tendency. In these unions, communists also had considerable influence. There also existed a great number of civic, educational and cultural organizations of a varied political and social nature. The cooperative movement, in which several million people were associated, constituted an important social and economic force.

National minority groups too, often discriminated against, took advantage of the right to cultivate their own institutions, social and cultural organizations, and political parties. The Jewish minority boasted particularly well-developed forms of collective life. They published their own newspapers, had a developed system of education on different levels, as well as economic organizations. Jewish theatres were of a high artistic standard and Jewish cultural centres in Poland were among the best organized in the world and displayed tremendous vitality. The Ukrainian cooperative movement was also highly successful. National minorities, the Ukrainians, Jews and Germans in particular, were well represented in the Seym. Just before the outbreak of war, however, many Polish citizens of German nationality succumbed to Nazi propaganda and joined the Nazi Fifth Column.

Many factors were responsible for Poland's political situation. After the death of Marshal Piłsudski, the ruling camp underwent a process of disintegration. Economic weakness, unresolved social and national conflicts and the tension resulting therefrom, hindered the ruling camp from winning over, or at least neutralizing, the broad masses. Under such conditions, the Right, as well as the Left opposition, constituted a force to be reckoned with. Polish democratic traditions, which were opposed to totalitarian methods of government, played an important part in this process. Inconsistencies in the actions of the ruling group, and even certain concessions resulted. Thus, for example, following the municipal elections announced shortly before the outbreak of war, the town council of Łódź, the second largest city in Poland, found itself in the hands of the Socialists.

The Growth of the German Threat. Polish Defensive Preparations

Germany's military potential was increasing. Hitler met no opposition by the Western nations in successively breaking the provisions of international treaties. Under these conditions, Poland found itself in a difficult situation; she maintained correct relations with the Germans, while simultaneously maintaining her ties with France. In 1936, when the German armies occupied the Rhineland, Poland expressed her readiness for military cooperation with France. France, however, which was pursuing a policy of appeasement, rejected the possibility of intervention. In the autumn of 1938 came the Munich Diktat, and as a result part of Czechoslovakia found itself in the hands of the Germans. The Polish government failed to see in the event a warning that the time had come for a basic reorientation in foreign policy, above all towards the USSR; instead she demanded by means of an ultimatum, as though associating herself with the signatories to the Munich agreement, the Czechoslovak region of Cieszyn Silesia. Shortly afterwards Poland herself became the object of German diplomatic offensives. The Germans proposed Poland's accession to the anti-Soviet, Anti-Comintern Pact, and demanded her agreement to the incorporation of Gdańsk into the Reich and the establishment of an extraterritorial German highway through Pomerania. Under these conditions Germany expressed her readiness to provide Poland with territorial guarantees and to extend the non-aggression pact for 25 years. These demands meant that Poland would become the target of the next German attack and Poland rejected them. The decision of the Polish government, which had the support of the whole population in the matter, was of historical importance. For the first time, Hitler encountered an obstacle on the path of his peaceful conquests. One can imagine the course events would have taken had Poland, with the sixth largest and strongest army in the world, decided to submit to German demands.

Simultaneously, preparations for the country's defence were intensified. Poland had been hastening modernization of her army since 1936 and building up an armaments industry, on which 40 per cent of the budget was spent. This was a tremendous effort, but owing to the country's economic weakness and the vast scale of the army's needs, the results achieved were incommensurate to demand, particularly as the full effects of modernization would not be felt till the beginning of the forties. Germany, which already had the most powerful army in the world, was spending almost thirty times as much as Poland on armaments.

On 15 March 1939, the Germans occupied the rest of Czechoslovakia. German soldiers stood along over 3,000 km. of Poland's frontiers (about 60 per cent of the total) and surrounded almost 70 per cent of Polish territory. In response to these moves, the Polish government ordered partial mobilization at the end of March. A Polish-British bilateral mutual aid declaration was announced on 6 April and joined by the French government. This meant that the beginning of a tripartite anti-German alliance had arisen in Europe. At the end of March, Hitler issued directives for the preparation of a campaign against Poland, and on 28 April abrogated the Polish-German declaration renouncing the use of force. The Germans intensified border provocations, increased their persecution of Poles in the Reich and Gdańsk, and also activated the pro-Hitler German Fifth Column in Poland. A protocol concerning the principles of joint operations on the part of the Polish and French armies in the event of war was signed in Paris on 19 May. However, Poland was unable to obtain concrete clarification on what these obligations consisted in. In the summer, negotiations took place between the USSR, France and Great Britain on military cooperation in case of German aggression. These negotiations did not yield any results. In the circumstance on 23 August, the USSR concluded a treaty with Germany. The Polish-British Treaty of Mutual Assistance was signed on 25 August.

Polish defensive preparations continued. Units for advanced defence position were secretly mobilized and posted to their respective areas. The airforce was moved to emergency airfields unknown to the enemy, to prevent planes being destroyed on the ground by surprise attack. General mobilization was proclaimed on 29 August; this applied to all reservists and subsidiary services. On the suggestion of the Allies, the order was countermanded and issued again a day later. This delay could not be undone. One day later, on the evening of 31 August, Germany broadcast a radio ultimatum to Poland, without even addressing it directly to the Polish government.

Poland During the Second World War (1939—45)

At 4 a.m. on the morning of 1 September 1939, German armies attacked Poland without a declaration of war. The Second World War had begun. Poland was invaded by one of the world's strongest and most modern armies. Over 1,800,000 soldiers, representing the élite of the German army, took part in the campaign against Poland. The Germans had about

9,000 guns, 2,500 modern tanks, and about 1,500 fighters and bombers. On the Polish side were 900,000 soldiers, grouped in 26 infantry divisions, eight cavalry brigades, three highland brigades and one motorized brigade, plus 56 under-equipped National Defence battalions. The Polish army had 3,000 guns, 475 tanks, mostly of the light reconnaissance type, and about 400 planes, of which 60 were modern bombers. Another 300,000 to 400,000 men for second-line formations were also mobilized.

The German army was vastly superior, mainly because of its tremendous fire-power and mobility due to its high standard of motorization. Like all aggressors, the Germans also had the superiority which the freedom to choose the time and place of attack always gives. Nonetheless, every German attack, some of them launched by surprise, encountered stubborn Polish resistance. The situation of the Polish Army was rendered all the more difficult by the new tactics of massed tank and motorized infantry attacks used by Germany for the first time in the Polish campaign. No successful defence against these tactics was evolved till the end of 1941, when Soviet troops on the outskirts of Moscow succeeded in stopping the German assault. For the first time too, the Luftwaffe launched massed air attacks on both military and civilian objectives. The German methods of warfare, conducted on Hitler's orders, were contrary to the conventions of international law. Countless thousands of defenceless civilians were killed in bombings and straffings by German airmen.

Up to 3 September, fighting continued along the main Polish line of defence, then Polish troops fell back on the main defences in heavy fighting, suffering severe losses. The main defence line ran from the North along the rivers Biebrza, Narew, Vistula and Brda, through Bydgoszcz, then along the Upper Noteć and Upper Warta in the vicinity of Łódź, through Silesia and down to the Carpathians. When it proved impossible to hold this line as planned, the Commander-in-Chief, Marshal Edward Śmigły-Rydz, ordered further retreat in a south-easterly direction, thinking that it would be possible to re-establish a united front. Up to 6 September, stubborn fighting continued in Pomerania, in the fiercely contested bloody battle of Mława, in the Łódź region, in Silesia and South of Cracow. The heroic defence of Westerplatte in Gdańsk, where a Polish outpost under two-hundred strong successfully repulsed for a week attacks launched by vastly superior enemy forces supported by artillery, air bombardment and naval guns (including the battleship Schleswig-Holstein), has gone in history.

On 3 September 1939, in fulfilment of their obligations to Poland, Britain and France declared war on Germany. The war had now become a coaliton operation. Though from the political point of view this was an event of supreme importance, it had no effect on Poland's military situation. Fighting alone and unaided, Poland had to face more than two thirds of the German military might.

On 8 September, fighting reached the outskirts of Warsaw; gradually German troops converged on the capital from every side. Heavy fighting was continuing in the central and southern regions of the country. The next stage of military operations opened on 9 September with a great Polish offensive in the Bzura River area, in which one third of the entire Polish army took part and which came to be known as the battle of Kutno. In this operation, commanded by General Tadeusz Kutrzeba, Polish divisions won important successes at first, but after a few days of heavy fighting the Germans regained the initiative; about 20 September, this greatest and most bloody battle of the Polish campaign ended in the routing of most of the Polish units taking part. This stage of the fighting ended with the defeat of a Polish army on the San in the South and the closing of the German pincer movement on the river Bug.

On 17 September, the Soviet Army crossed the Polish frontier. On the night of 17/18 September, the president of the republic, the government and the High Command, stationed during the last few days in a command-post close to the Romanian border, crossed the frontier and left Polish territory.

The fighting, however, continued. In the city and port of Gdynia, the struggle went on until 18 September. Lvov, surrounded by the Germans, resisted successfully till 22 September, when the officer in charge of defence surrendered the city to the Soviet army. In the Lublin region, two great battles were fought in the Tomaszów area on 26 September. Short of ammunition, and after exhausting all the possibilities of defence, Warsaw surrendered on 28 September. Apart from regular troops under the command of General Juliusz Rommel, volunteer units which included many workers, socialists and communists, had also fought in defence of the capital.

Stefan Starzyński, the Mayor of Warsaw, was the heart and soul of the capital's defence. Arrested by the Germans immediately after occupation of the city, he was murdered some time later in unexplained circumstances. The fort of Modlin surrendered on 29 September and the Hel Peninsula on 1 October. The last great battle of the campaign, under the command of General Franciszek Kleeberg, was Kock fought between 2 and 5 October.

The military and political significance of the September campaign was considerable. For the first time Hitler had met with resistance which led to the formation of a coalition which after five years was to destroy the Axis Powers. Hitler's plan to conquer Poland in a lightning campaign failed. The campaign in Poland lasted five weeks. After the first week's fighting, the Polish side temporarily gained a strategic initiative. German losses were serious: over 40,000 battle casualties, about 500 planes shot down, almost a thousand tanks and self-propelled guns destroyed and quantities of various other equipment destroyed or damaged. These losses were roughly equivalent to the losses suffered by Germany in all campaigns fought on land up to the attack on the Soviet Union. In effect, the Allies gained six months time in which to prepare for the defence of the Western front. They also gained inestimable knowledge about the German *Blitzkrieg* tactics. Unfortunately, they made no use of this experience, just as they had failed to take advantage of the opportunity offered them in September 1939, when the bulk of German forces was committed in Poland.

The Nazis occupied a territory of 188,700 sq. km., with a population of 22 million, including 18.5 million Poles, 2.5 million Jews and under a million Germans. The area incorporated into the USSR amounted to 201,000 sq. km., with a population of some 13 million, of which the majority were Ukrainians, Byelorussians and Jews, with the Poles numbering about 5 million.

The Germans divided the occupied territory into two zones. The Poznań voivodship, Pomerania, a considerable part of the Warsaw and Łódź voivodships, part of the Kielce voivodship (Dabrowa Coal Basin) and of Cracow voivodship, and Silesia were incorporated in the Reich. A great many Poles were summarily deported from this zone, many were sent to Germany for compulsory labour. The rest of Polish territory under German occupation was formed into the so-called Government General. According to German plans, this area constituted a temporary reservation for Poles and was subjected to extraordinarily brutal economic exploitation and terror.

Already during the fighting of 1939 the Nazis proceeded with exterminating the Polish population. Immediately after the end of the fighting, tens of thousands of Poles were murdered in Bydgoszcz, and the first mass execution of 107 Poles took place in Wawer near Warsaw over Christmas 1939. Political and cultural activities were forbidden, secondary schools, colleges and universities were closed down and the work of elementary schools was greatly restricted. The bestial treatment of the professors of the Jagiellonian University in Cracow shocked Europe. The Germans gathered 183 scholars in the university building ostensibly in order to listen to a lecture on German science, after which they were deported to the concentration camp of Sachsenhausen, where many of them died.

The first victims of extermination were eminent politicians. The leader of the Peasant Party, Maciej Rataj, and Mieczysław Niedziałkowski, leader of the Socialists, were killed in Palmiry near Warsaw. To this day, the place where Warsaw's heroic mayor Stefan Starzyński was murdered has not been established.

Mass round-ups of civilians in the streets served as a means of gaining free labour; about three million people were deported to Germany as slave labourers. Civilians stopped at random were shot in public executions or sent to concentration camps. In Auschwitz alone between 2.8 million (according to the Supreme National Tribunal in Poland) and 4 million (according to the Soviet Extraordinary State Commission for the investigation of Nazi crimes in Auschwitz) perished in gas chambers and executions or else as a result of starvation, back-breaking labour and disease. In 1940, the occupation authorities established special ghettos for the Jews, where they were gradually deprived of the means of livelihood and starved. However, as the Germans considered that the Jews were dying off too slowly, they proceeded to murder them outright, either on the spot or in special camps. Of over three million Polish Jews, only a very small proportion survived; these owed their lives to Poles who supplied food to the ghettos and hid escaping Jews, despite the fact that this was punishable by death. A Council of Aid for the Jews was formed — a special body which grouped together numerous Polish organizations in helping the Jewish population. Beginning in 1942, the Polish government in London took various steps to inform the world of the heinous crimes perpetrated on Polish Jews by the Nazis and demanded that measures should be taken to prevent mass genocide and punish those guilty.

Methods of total extermination were used by the Nazis towards all Poles. Every day thousands of defenceless people were killed in towns and villages and perished in concentration camps. In the course of the so-called pacification operations, the populations of hundreds of villages were wiped out, especially in the Zamość region, and in Warsaw after the liquidation of the 1944 Uprising. In all, over six million Poles lost their lives at the hands of the Nazis.

The Polish population did not become reconciled to defeat. Several thousand soldiers made their way via Hungary and Romania to France, where a new government was formed under General Sikorski. At the same time Sikorski became commander-in-chief of the reorganized Polish Army in the West. In accordance with an agreement concluded with the government, a Polish Army of four divisions plus several air fighter squadrons were formed in France. An Independent Carpathian Rifle Brigade was formed in Syria. Polish ships which reached Britain either before the war or already during hostilities went to make up the core of the Polish Navy in Great Britain. Efforts were made to build up a Polish Air Force. At that time the Polish armies in the West totalled some 80,000. In May and June 1940 the Independent Podhale Rifle Brigade as well as four Polish warships, took part in the Norwegian campaign, including the Battle of Narvik. All units formed in France, troops evacuated from Norway, and Polish aircraft took part in the defence of France in May an June 1940 and following its defeat were mostly dispersed after putting up last-stand resistance. Thanks to British assistance, some 23,000 troops were evacuated to Britain where a 1st Polish Corps was formed. The latter was stationed in Scotland, initially as defence against German invasion. The first Polish fighter squadrons to be formed in Britain, 302 and 303, fought in the Battle of Britain between August and 31 October 1940. Of the total of 1733 enemy planes shot down in this period, Polish airmen were responsible for 250. The contribution of the Polish Navy in this and further stages of the war was considerable. It participated in 1162 operations, escorted 787 convoys, sunk at least nine enemy warships and possibly a further five, 39 cargo ships and carriers, damaged 19 vessels and downed 30 aircraft.

The Independent Carpathian Rifle Brigade, which had been withdrawn from Syria after the capitulation of France and which at the time numbered over 5,000 troops, fought at the side of the British in North Africa between October 1940 and March 1942 and won fame in the defence of Tobruk.

Following German aggression against the USSR, relations with that country were re-established. In accord to a political and military agreement a Polish army began to be formed in the USSR. The Polish community in the USSR included resettled Poles and POWs who were given amnesty. Several Polish divisions were formed. As a result of the stand taken by the Polish government-in-exile in London, supported by the British and Americans, these units — numbering some 40,000 troops — were evacuated to the Middle East and there transformed into the 2nd Polish Corps under the command of General Władysław Anders. This corps fought on the Italian front and made its name in the capture of Monte Cassino in May 1944 and Ancona and in the fighting at Bologna.

The 1st corps fought in France, Belgium and the Netherlands, and later in Germany. The 1st Armoured Division under General Stanisław Maczek played an important role in the battle of Falaise. General Sosabowski's 1st Independent Parachute Brigade took part in the battle of Arnhem, the largest air landing operation in the Second World War. Polish units also participated in operations conducted by the French resistance.

In the final stage of the war the Polish Armed Forces in the West totalled some 220,000 troops, including 14 air squadrons and 15 larger and several smaller warships. Polish airmen shot down a thousand enemy aircraft and some 200 V missiles while Polish bombers performed about 12,000 missions against the enemy. Thus the Polish contribution to the war effort was by no means negligible.

A resistance movement grew up in Poland itself in the first days of the occupation. Immediately after the September campaign, army units undertook partisan actions. The most famous was the detachment under Major Henryk Dobrzański, whose *nom de guerre* was Hubal, which operated in the Świętokrzyskie Mountains until the end of April 1940. On 26 September 1939, the command of besieged Warsaw formed a secret military organization, the Service for Polish Victory, transformed into the Armed Combat Union (ZWZ) in 1940, and finally into the mass underground organization called the Home Army (1942). Its successive commanders were General Stefan Rowecki ("Grot") and General Tadeusz Komorowski ("Bór"). The Home Army, which was subordinated to the government-in-exile in London, was the latter's military base in Poland. The government was supported by the pre-war opposition parties, which now continued their activities underground. They included: (1) the National Party (its extreme Right Wing was in opposition to the government, while its military organization, the National Armed Forces, more than once actively opposed the progressive forces); (2) the Labour Party and the Polish Socialist Party (whose faction cooperating with the government was called Freedom, Equality, Independence); and (3) the Peasant Party, the best organized and most influential of the parties (its military organization was known as the Peasant Battalions, which were partially taken over by the command of the Home Army as a result of a later consolidation). On the basis of these groupings and several smaller ones a network of organs known as the Home Delegate's Office of the Government-in-Exile was formed. In accordance with a tradition dating from the January Insurrection, these organizations, which existed at a central and a local level, were known as the Underground State.

Forms of resistance varied and included the preparation and undertaking of armed combat, diversion and sabotage. The attitude of Polish society, which was proud of the fact that it had produced no quisling and was not stigmatized by organized collaboration, was influenced by the various underground institutions. These included secret newspapers (some were published in tens of thousands of copies and the number of titles reached a thousand) which reached all parts of the country and even prisoner-of-war and concentration camps. Artistic and scientific activity, officially prohibited by the Nazis, was cultivated in secret. Alongside newspapers and leaflets, serious literature and school textbooks were also published. A network of secret schools sprang up. In Warsaw, the University of the Western Territories and other institutions of higher learning carried on illegal teaching activity. Almost all the secondary schools which had existed before the war, functioned underground. In the field of public schooling in the Government General, secret supplementary teaching of subjects connected with Polish life was given to about a million pupils and was conducted by 19,000 teachers. Secret education included about

100,000 secondary school pupils and over 10,000 university students. Underground teaching also existed in the areas incorporated in the Reich.

It would be difficult to enumerate the victims who fell on this and other "civilian" fronts. The Nazis were unable, however, to abolish intellectual life in Poland, or to reduce the Polish nation to the level of slaves. Communists were found in the front line of battle. They participated in the Workers' Battalions in Defence of Warsaw, and Marian Buczek, a communist released from prison who lost his life while leading a group of soldiers in the attempt to break through to embattled Warsaw, became a symbol of the communists' attitude. A dozen or more communist groups were formed after 1939 (the Hammer and Sickle, the Proletarian, the Bulletin Group) to carry out political and military activities. These organizations, along with the "Initiative Group", formed in the USSR with the help of the Communist International, led to the formation of the Polish Workers' Party (PPR) on 5 January 1942. The Party put forward the idea of a national front which would unite patriotic forces and pointed out the need for mass armed combat. In its proposals, it harked back to the revolutionary traditions of the Polish proletariat, especially to the successes of the Communist Party of Poland during its struggles for the establishment of a popular front in Poland. The First Secretary of the Central Committee of the Polish Workers' Party was Marceli Nowotko; after his death, he was succeeded by Paweł Finder who was followed by Władysław Gomułka after Finder's arrest. The Polish Workers' Party formed its own military organization, the People's Guard, whose chief-of-staff was Franciszek Jóźwiak.

After the Nazi invasion of the USSR in June 1941, Poland became the immediate rear area of the new theatre of war, and this stimulated demonstrations against the occupation forces while sabotage and diversion increased. Polish-Soviet diplomatic relations were re-established in 1941.

The establishment of diplomatic relations with the Soviet government met with a hostile reception among some sections of the London camp, especially among the former supporters of the *Sanacja*, headed by General Kazimierz Sosnkowski. The Polish Soviet agreement was, however, in line with conceptions of the Polish Workers' Party, which at that time began talks with the representatives of the London government in Poland. These talks yielded no results. This coincided with the severing of diplomatic relations between the Soviet government and the Polish government-in-exile in London. After the tragic death of General Sikorski (4 July 1943), the international position of this government, which then became headed by Stanisław Mikołajczyk, the Peasant Party leader, was further weakened. This was also a result of events in Poland, where the Polish Workers' Party gained in influence and detachments of the People's Guard became increasingly active.

In 1943 there arose in the USSR on the initiative of Polish communists, the Union of Polish Patriots, headed by the well-known writer and political leader, Wanda Wasilewska. Under its patronage, the First "Tadeusz Kościuszko" Infantry Division (commanded by General Zygmunt Berling) was organized in the USSR, with the agreement of the Soviet government. The first battle with German forces, fought by this division at Lenino (12 October 1943), began a long series of battles waged by the Polish People's Army (in People's Poland, the anniversary of the Battle of Lenino is commemorated as Army Day). The 1st Corps of the Polish Armed Forces was formed in the USSR in August 1943, and later transformed into the Polish First Army in the spring of 1944. This Army cooperated with the Soviet Army in the liberation of Poland and then participated in the successive Soviet offensives culminating in the storming of Berlin.

In the final stage of the war, the Polish People's Army totalled some 400,000 men, while the Polish Army in the West numbered over 200,000. To those figures must be added the partisan units of the Polish resistance movement. Thus the Polish people made a great contribution to the Allied victory.

On 31 December 1943, in cooperation with members of the left wings of the Socialist, Peasant and Democratic Parties the Polish Workers' Party established a kind of underground Parliament, the National Home Council. In its first documents the National Home Council proclaimed the restoration of independent Poland as a country of social justice and a democratic political system, in which the working masses would exercise decisive influence on the functioning of the state. Far reaching social reforms were promised, first and foremost an agrarian reform. Foreign policy would be based on friendship and cooperation with the USSR, founded on justice and the settlement of the territorial conflict in the East on the strength of ethnical criteria. The document also announced the restoration of

Poland's former Piast territories in the North and West. Declaring itself as the supreme authority in the future independent Poland, the National Home Council refused the London Government and its representations in Poland the right to represent the country's interests. The National Home Council also transformed the People's Guard into the People's Army and appointed General Michał Rola-Zymierski as its commanding officer. In answer to a call by the National Home Council, a clandestine network of people's councils began to be formed in Poland.

The formation of the National Home Council meant that a centre of revolutionary authority had been established in the occupied country which had assumed responsibility for Poland's future. The Union of Polish Patriots and units of the Polish First Army in the USSR fighting on the Eastern front recognized the National Home Council as the supreme Polish authority. The Soviet Union also recognized it as the supreme authority of the independent Polish state. All this established grounds for the assumption of power in liberated Poland by forces connected with the revolutionary movement.

In 1943 important battles were waged by the partisans with Nazi troops, for example, at Zaboreczno (the Peasant Battalions), in Parczew Forest (the People's Guard), and Siekierzyński Forest (the Home Army). In response to the Nazi decision to proceed to the final liquidation of the Warsaw ghetto, an uprising broke out in the ghetto in April 1943. During the fighting, which lasted for several weeks, the insurgents benefited from material and military aid given by Polish underground organizations. After the collapse of the uprising, the Nazis deported the remaining Jews to extermination camps and demolished or set fire to all the buildings.

Sabotage continued, especially attacks on German rail transport and the destruction of rolling stock. The Polish resistance movement obtained a prototype of the German V-1 missile and sent it to Great Britain; they killed many Nazi criminals in spectacular operations, such as the hangman of occupied Europe, SS General Kutschera. Partisan battles intensified in spring 1944. The largest partisan battle on Polish territory took place in the Solska Forest (9—25 June 1944). Tens of thousands of partisans fought in forest detachments and the occupying forces had to deploy 100,000 soldiers to cope with them. The resistance movement numbered up to half a million participants.

The threat this army represented forced the enemy to maintain an occupation army of several hundred thousand men.

Andrzej Ajnenkiel

Liberation of Poland. Formation of the New Political Model of the State. The End of the Second World War

As the Soviet troops were approaching the Polish-Soviet frontier of 1939 (they crossed that line on the night of 3 January 1944) the Polish government in London, headed by Stanisław Mikołajczyk, and in particular the General Command of the Home Army, voiced their protest against the establishment of the future Polish eastern frontier on the Curzon line, that is, along the Bug. Nonetheless, these recommendations were put forward at the first conference of Roosevelt, Churchill, and Stalin as the leaders of the anti-Nazi coalition, held in Teheran at the turn of November 1943. Reference was then also made to the moving of Poland's future western frontier to the Odra. Mikołajczyk's protests were, accordingly, at variance with the main lines of the Great Powers' policies. Mikołajczyk failed to win British support on the issue and Churchill stated that this plan would be the solution of the Polish issue on a large scale. Nor was Mikołajczyk successful in his talks with Stalin. The Polish emigré authorities then tried to put into effect their plan known under the code name *Burza* (Storm). According to this plan, the Home Army and delegates of the Polish government-in-exile were to take over civilian and military power in the territories between the Polish-Soviet frontier of 1939 and the Curzon Line before the Soviet troops could enter them. This, too, failed to win the support of the Western Powers.

Sosnkowski then proposed to use the Home Army for a new operation, this time directed against the Soviet troops, but his idea was not supported by the emigré government which had been reorganized in the meantime. While all this was going on, the Poeple's Army, the Peasant Battalions, and other minor organizations were active behind the front-line, accompanied by some detachments of the Home Army.

The aim of the emigré government was to have at least the territories to the west of the Curzon line liberated with the participation of its troops, and hence the Polish government adopted a double course. On the one hand, it organized an uprising in Warsaw to liberate the city before this could be done by the Soviet troops (which had, in the meantime, reached the Vistula). But these troops, having advanced on the so-called Byelorussian front for 500 kilometres instead of the 250 originally planned, needed much time to prepare for a new offensive, the more so as they had encountered stubborn German resistance which General Komorowski, the commander of the Home Army, did not consider since he counted on the Soviet Army crossing the Vistula. At this time, Mikołajczyk paid his next visit to Moscow as he wanted to conclude an agreement on the take-over by the emigré government of the territories liberated by the Soviet Army. The taking of Warsaw, which was planned by the London government as a relatively short campaign, was to be his trump card.

The Warsaw Uprising, which — contrary to the opinion of some leading representatives of Polish emigré circles in Britain — broke out on 1 August 1944, was brutally suppressed. It was, nevertheless, a great demonstration of patriotism on the part of both the Home Army and other groups (including the Warsaw group of the People's Army whose commander, Bolesław Kowalski, lost his life in Warsaw) and the civilian population. Everybody expected the liberation and wanted to expedite it; it was also believed that the Uprising had been well prepared both militarily and politically. But in fact it had no chance of success — even though the Soviet and Polish troops after heavy fighting occupied Praga (the part of Warsaw on the east bank of the Vistula). The Uprising lasted 63 days and cost the lives of some 200,000 Poles of whom some 22,000 were soldiers. The German losses amounted to about 26,000 while the losses of the Soviet air force in the region of Warsaw were about 250 men, of whom about 100 were Poles. Following a direct order from Hitler, about 80 per cent of the city of Warsaw, including many treasures of Polish culture, was destroyed.

The plans of the Polish emigré government were collapsing even regardless of the disaster in Warsaw. There was already in Poland an organized centre of power which had to be reckoned with because it enjoyed the support of the Soviet Union. In March 1944 the National Home Council approached the Soviet government and the Union of Polish Patriots through its representatives in Moscow and obtained Stalin's approval to set up the Office of the National Home Council's Delegates for the Liberated Areas. This was made easier by Mikołajczyk himself, who — counting in vain on the support this time of the United States — refused all compromise with the National Home Council.

When the Soviet troops liberated Chełm, the first major town to the West of the Curzon line, the Office of the National Home Council's Delegates for the Liberated Areas converted itself into the Polish Committee of National Liberation (21 July 1944), and the next day, issued its Manifesto. The Polish Committee of National Liberation, in which the Polish Workers' Party played the principal role, had in its programme the restoration of the 1921 Constitution, cooperation with the Soviet Union and acceptance of the recommendations concerning Poland's frontiers put forward at the Teheran conference. It also proceeded immediately to offer full assistance to the Red Army and had all the liberated areas working for the army. The Polish First Army and the People's Army were merged into the uniform Polish Army. At the same time the Polish Second Army and other units were being formed in the liberated areas. The Polish Committee of National Liberation, functioning as a provisional government, took Lublin as its headquarters. During his talks in Moscow in August 1944, Mikołajczyk rejected Bierut's proposals (to be himself prime minister and to allocate three posts in a joint cabinet) as he still counted upon the success of the Warsaw Uprising which had broken out only ten days earlier.

Between July 1944 and January 1945, when the new Soviet offensive began, the Polish Committee of National Liberation was engaged in direct activity in the liberated territories (those to the east of the Vistula). The Peasant Party and the Polish Socialist Party were reconstructed (the latter on the basis of its former left wing), and the same applied to the trade unions and youth organizations. The Polish Workers' Party and the Polish Socialist Party became mass organizations. Local self-government (people's councils) was set up, and the police and security forces were established. A decree on agrarian reform was issued and its enforcement began immediately; the reform covered land which had previously been owned by the State, by Germans, and by people who held estates of 50 hectares or more (in the Western territories the lower limit was 100 hectares). This meant the elimination from the social structure of the class of owners of large estates. At the same time, partisan warfare intensified in the areas still occupied by the Germans; these regions were also penetrated by Soviet reconnaissance groups, which availed themselves of the assistance of the local population.

In the meantime, negotiations concerning the future Polish government were continuing, but no agreement was reached in the talks held on 13—14 October 1944; the emigré government in London refused to make concessions on the issue of Poland's eastern frontiers, despite the lack of support by Churchill and Roosevelt; Mikołajczyk, considered to have been too conciliatory, had to resign and the new cabinet, headed by Tomasz Arciszewski, proved even less flexible. Wincenty Witos, already gravely ill, who was to have been brought to London, was then another candidate for prime minister of the emigré cabinet. There was also a campaign for the international recognition of the Polish Committee of National Liberation. Polish organizations which supported that political body were formed in France and Belgium.

On 31 December 1944, the National Home Council appointed the Provisional Government of the Republic of Poland, recognized by the Soviet Union, with which that government signed, on 21 April 1945, the Treaty of Friendship, Mutual Aid and Post-war Cooperation (to be in force for 20 years and subject to prolongation). This signing took place after the next Big Three Conference, held at Yalta on 4—11 February 1945, which confirmed Poland's eastern frontier on the Curzon line, spoke about the necessity of adding to Poland territories of a considerable area in the West and in the North, and demanded the establishment of a government of national unity that would enjoy the support of the Western Powers. Agreement was finally reached at a new conference in Moscow: a Provisional Government of National Unity was formed, with Edward Osóbka-Morawski as prime minister and Władysław Gomułka and Stanisław Mikołajczyk as his deputies. The Polish Workers' Party and the Polish Socialist Party received nearly two thirds of the portfolios, the rest going to the Peasant Party and the Democratic Party. The state of specific biarchy came to an end, and an amnesty was proclaimed for those who had participated in the conspiracy that supported the emigré government in London.

The liberation of the whole country followed the above-mentioned Soviet offensive (started in January 1945). The Polish First Army took part in breaking through the so-called Pomeranian Wall, in reconquering Kołobrzeg, Gdynia, and Gdańsk, and in the Battle of Berlin. The Second Army, led by General Świerczewski, at first moved toward Pomerania and later turned in the direction of Dresden and was engaged in the Battle of Bautzen, important for the taking of Berlin; it also took part in the Prague campaign and liberated a number of places in Czechoslovakia. In spite of imminent defeat, the Germans to the last moment continued to exterminate Poles.

New organization of normal life, protection of national property, putting factories into operation, opening schools and launching cultural undertakings accompanied the liberation of towns and rural areas. Nuclei of local power were set up before contacts with the central authorities could be established, which, however, happened quickly. The hard work on the reconstruction of the country began.

Poland's western frontiers were fixed in Potsdam (17 July to 2 August 1945) at the Conference of Prime Ministers of the Three Allied Powers — the USSR, Great Britain and the US. The Polish delegation with Bolesław Bierut was also present. It was decided that the remaining German population (most Germans had fled to the West before the arrival of the Soviet army) would be transferred from Poland and other countries to Germany.

Birth of the Polish People's Republic.
Reconstruction. The First Reforms.
Stabilization of People's Rule

Poland suffered enormous losses during the Second World War. While in 1939 Poland had 35.1 million inhabitants, the census of 14 February 1946 showed only 23.9 million inhabitants instead of the expected ca. 40 million. The losses in national resources amounted to about 38 per cent. The Polish nation was faced with the extremely difficult task of reconstruction, which did not mean simply the return to previous conditions because these reflected backwardness inherited from the past and not fully eliminated in the period between the two World Wars: Poland, then, was still a backward agricultural country with an obsolete social structure, marked by only small participation in culture by a large proportion of the population, especially in the rural areas. The wounds inflicted by the war brought all those problems into sharp focus.

The nation and the State authorities were faced with a task of historic significance: reconstruction had to be combined with restructuring the national economy and society, and also with shaping a new mode of cultural life. In the first post-war years the principal task was to reconstruct the areas which had earlier formed parts of Germany, namely Silesia, Eastern Pomerania, the region of the middle Odra, Warmia, and Mazuria, and also to stabilize the power taken over by the left. The ethnic unity of the population, resulting from the shifting of the frontiers, proved conducive to this process. Conditions were also secured for a new settlement of the relations between State and Church. Poland now had an area of 312,700 sq. kilometres, one third of which consisted of the said regions in the West and North and the area of the former Free City of Gdańsk. Even though the area of the State was reduced by 77,000 sq. kilometres the conditions for industrialization were now much better: the territories in the West and in the North, now incorporated into Poland, had in 1937 an industrial production that amounted to from 60 to 70 per cent of the entire industrial output of pre-war Poland, while the analogous figure for the territories to the East of the Bug was merely 12 to 13 per cent. The disposition of the national resources in the newly incorporated regions helped the process of economic reconstruction.

The implementation of the immense tasks which the reconstruction of the country involved was, for the period of over one year immediately after the termination of the war, intertwined with the new government's struggle for the stabilization of its power. This was made even more difficult by the fact that a considerable part of society, despite marked general radicalization during the war, was still mistrustful of the new government, and that attitude was to change only in the process of reconstruction and — at the same time — the shaping of a new life. The refusal by Britain and the United States to recognize the emigré government in Lodon certainly did help in that process, but, on the other hand, the fact that Mikołajczyk became a member of the cabinet at home meant that the struggle for power was to continue. Mikołajczyk, in his striving to secure a social basis for his political activity, tried to become the leader of the entire peasant movement. When he failed to dominate the leftist Peasant Party, founded on 25—26 March 1945, he formed his own party, called the Polish Peasant Party (22 August 1945). Paradoxically, this became an opposition party within the government and at the same time the centre of those forces which were openly hostile to the new political and social system. Many members of the Polish Peasant Party had nothing in common with the peasants. The National Democratic Party also tried to renew its activity.

The liberation of Poland by the Red Army was decisive for the left, keeping the power in its hand, and the presence of Soviet troops in the country prevented a civil war from breaking out (even though there was some fighting in certain regions). The first post-war period witnessed the great battle of classes which was decisive in the struggle for power. The people's power was opposed by both the political underground, consisting partly of members of Polish organizations active during the war (for example, those members of the Home Army who did not recognize the dissolution of that organization in August 1945), and by the legal opposition consisting of various social groups; it is to be noted that in some cases the demarcation line between the legal and the illegal opposition was rather difficult to draw.

Suppression of the armed underground movement was not an easy task. Between 22 July 1944, and 1 January 1946, members of the armed underground killed more than 7,000 people, primarily local activists of the Polish Workers' Party, militiamen, officers and soldiers of the Polish Army, and members of the security forces. There were more victims later because the armed underground movement was finally suppressed only in 1947. At the same time the struggle against the Ukrainian nationalists and pro-Nazi organizations which called themselves the Ukrainian Insurgent Army went on for three years mainly in the south-eastern part of the country.

The Polish Peasant Party (PSL) advocated the solution that was termed agrarianism, that is a capitalistic political system based on a peasant party and having the features of parliamentary democracy. Hence the main catchword of the Polish Peasant Party was "the defence of democracy", which repudiated the values of the emergent socialist model of the State, in which power was to be wielded by the working class in an alliance with the peasants, the petty bourgeoisie and the intelligentsia. The PSL did not in principle come out against the reforms (the nationalization of industry and agrarian reform), because that would not have been supported by the majority of the population. But the PSL nevertheless overestimated its own strength. In the referendum held on 30 June 1946, before the elections to the Seym, victory went to the bloc of the democratic parties, consisting of the Polish Workers' Party, the Polish Socialist Party, the Peasant Party, and the Democratic Party. Attendance at the polls was 85.8 per cent. In reply to the first question: "Are you for the abolition of the Senate?" the "ayes" accounted for 68.2 per cent of the replies. Their number was 77.3 per cent in the case of the second question, namely that concerning the approval of the nationalization of industry and of the agrarian reforms, and 91.4 per cent in the case of the third question, namely that about the fixing of the Polish western frontier along the Baltic coast, the Odra, and the Lusatian Nysa. The Polish Peasant Party, which recommended a "no" answer to the first question, thus won only 31.8 per cent of the votes.

Its defeat was even greater in the elections to the Seym, held on 19 January 1947: the PSL received only 10.3 per cent of the votes, which secured it merely 28 seats. Mikołajczyk's opposition was thus eliminated as a major political force, and he himself fled the country in October 1947 to join the emigré government in London. Bolesław Bierut was elected the president of the Republic of Poland, while the cabinet had Józef Cyrankiewicz (Polish Socialist Party) as prime minister, Władysław Gomułka (Polish Workers' Party) as the first deputy prime minister and Antoni Korzycki (Peasant Party) as the second deputy prime minister. The Seym passed what was currently called the Short Constitution, replaced by the full Constitution on 22 July 1952; according to the latter "Poland is a people's democracy" and power belongs to the working people of town and country, through their representatives elected to the Seym and people's councils in universal, equal, direct and secret suffrage.

An essential step in the consolidation of the people's rule consisted in the unification of the worker movement, which took place in 1948. The Polish Workers' Party, which in December 1948 had over one million members (as compared with 800,000 in 1947 and 235,000 in 1945), merged with the Polish Socialist Party, which had over 500,000 members and revealed a strong tendency to grow, to form the Polish United Workers' Party (PZPR). The youth organizations also merged into the Union of Polish Youth (ZMP). This did not take place without discussions concerning the political programme of the new party: it envisaged the construction of a socialist system on the basis of a broad front of national unity. The Jewish Socialist Party (the Bund) also acceded to the PZPR and the peasant movement was reorganized in 1949, becoming the United Peasant Party (ZSL). The Labour Party was dissolved after a short period of existence, and the bloc of the democratic parties included the PZPR, ZSL and the Democratic Party (SD), the latter two recognizing the leading role of the former and acting as its allies.

It is to be noted that essential political divergences developed within the Polish Workers' Party several months before the fusion of the two worker parties. The controversy was over the attitude to be adopted toward the decisions — passed by the Information Bureau of the Communist and Workers' Parties that had replaced the Communist International — concerning the collectivization of agriculture in people's democracies, the situation within the Communist Party of Yugoslavia (which opposed the Stalin cult), and also the assessment of the traditions of the Polish worker movement. In the atmosphere which then prevailed in the worker movement, dominated by the dogmatic personality cult, those who opposed uniformity in the methods of building socialism and saw the necessity of taking the distinctive national features into account were easily labelled "rightist" and "nationalist deviationists". They included a group of prominent party leaders with Władysław Gomułka, who was expelled from the party authorities in 1949. The resolution concerned with the rightist and nationalist deviation was revoked in October 1956, and formally rescinded at the Third Congress of the Polish United Workers' Party in 1959.

At the time of the struggle for the stabilization of the people's rule, basic social and economic reforms were being carried out. There were also large-scale migrations, due not only to the shifting of the Polish frontiers but also to the population movements that had taken place during the Second World War. All this was accompanied by the reconstruction of the war-devastated country.

The agrarian reform was continued in the territories to the West of the Vistula as soon as these were liberated. Those peasants who did not receive plots because of a shortage of land in the area were advised to move to the western and the northern territories. The decree on the agrarian reform of 6 September 1944 transferred over 6 million hectares of land to over one million peasant families. 814,000 new farms were formed and 254,400 existing ones were expanded.

There were, it is true, considerable differences in the way the agrarian reform was carried out in the various regions, for example in Little Poland, which did not, however, alter the social status of that population. In Great Poland and in Pomerania, where there was more land, obtaining it as a result of the agrarian reform often meant social promotion. On the whole, the size of the new farms was primarily determined by the size of a given family. In Great Poland and in Pomerania smallholders tended to form cooperative farms but the authorities at that time did not support such undertakings, in order to avoid the impression that agriculture was going to be collectivized after the Soviet pattern.

The agrarian reform was connected with migrations, especially to the territories regained in the West and the North, where by the end of 1947 over two million people had settled, nearly one half of them being Poles resettled from the territories to the east of the Bug. The agrarian reform led to the emergence of many independent farms: nearly 22 farms out of every 100 private farms originated totally or in part from the agrarian reform and the shifting of the population. There was also a novel element in the structure of agriculture in the form of the State Farms, which by 1950 had covered about nine per cent of all agricultural land (ca. 2,200,000 hectares). Some 3.5 million hectares of forests were nationalized, which made it possible to cultivate the forest more rationally than previously.

The situation of the rural population after the war was far from good: 354,000 farmsteads were destroyed, there were shortages of farm animals (including draught animals), fertilizers, and implements. In 1946 the level of agricultural production was only about two thirds of that in 1937. To ensure food supplies to the towns, compulsory deliveries of agricultural produce by the farmers were introduced for a certain period. The ratio of prices also was bad for the farmers, bacause the prices of industrial goods were very high, following the destruction of numerous factories. Loans for the reconstruction of farms were provided by the State. The rural population was greatly differentiated and not free from internal conflicts. At first strong differences were felt between the old residents in a given area, on the one hand, and those who had settled there as repatriates or migrants, on the other, but the adaptation of the latter groups to the new conditions was quick, which led to the integration of the rural population in the various regions. Until about 1948 there was little marriage between those groups, but gradually this changed. On the whole, the social position of the peasants improved and this gradually began to influence their political attitudes: the political self-consciousness of the peasant was determined by such new criteria as the origin of his farm (inherited, acquired as a result of the agrarian reform, etc.) and the political traditions of his family, rather, than by the mere size of his farm. An important role was played in this respect by the abolition in 1946 of the compulsory deliveries of agricultural produce, better supplies of industrial goods, the decline of the importance of the Polish Peasant Party, and the collapse of the militant underground movement. It is to be noted, however, that compulsory deliveries were reintroduced at the time of the great industrialization drive in 1951 (cereals) and in 1952 (pigs and milk).

The development of industry, which after its nationalization passed into the hands of the State except for small workshops, was also far from easy. The devastations had been immense: by 1945 148,000 (305 million cu. metres) of all buildings had been destroyed in towns in the western and northern regions. Warsaw lay almost completely in ruins. (It is worth noting that Hans Frank during his first stay in Warsaw on 10 October 1939 personally helped destroy what had been left of the Throne Hall in the Royal Castle and that in November 1939 German officials were formally permitted to plunder the ruins of that castle for their private use). Harbours, most big bridges and high-tension lines, and many factories had been destroyed. In the mining, mineral, metallurgical, precision, electrical engineering, chemical, textile and building industries, the devastations accounted for 60 to 90 per cent.

Until the middle of 1945 the Polish national economy practically had all the features characteristic of war-time. The period from mid-1945 to the end of 1949 can be defined as that of economic stabilization and reconstruction based on short-term and long-term planning. The principal role was played in that respect by the economic reconstruction plan for 1947—49; particularly good results were obtained in the reconstruction of industry and land transport and in the maintenance of a balanced budget. The national income rose in that period by 45 per cent, which meant that the pre-war level was exceeded by 25 per cent and by some 36 per cent when calculated per capita. There were also visible changes in the structure of the process whereby that income was created: in 1949 the ratio of industrial to agricultural output was approximately 2:1, while in 1937 it was 1:1. Industrial production increased, as compared with 1937, by 76 per cent, that of hard coal twice, and that of electric power, 2.3 times.

Accelerated economic growth through industrialization was then achieved mainly by the maximum use made of manpower, that is, practically by the elimination of the latent unemployment in the rural areas, typical of the pre-war period, and less by increased labour productivity. Considerable exodus of people from country to town could be observed.

That town-ward flow of the population must be counted, next to repatriation from the eastern areas and migrations to the western and northern regions, among the greatest manifestations of vertical and horizontal social mobility in People's Poland. They were two processes of great significance for the country, which made it possible to incorporate the western and northern territories into the national economic system and to transform the country from a predominantly agricultural into a predominantly industrial one.

The number of people repatriated from the Soviet Union in 1944—48 amounted to over 1.5 million, while that of repatriates and re-emigrants from Germany and other countries was nearly 1.5 million between 1945 and 1948. All those Poles who found themselves in the Reich and in Austria (mainly as forced labour deportees) were repatriated during 1945. The converse process, that is the return of aliens to their respective countries. was on a much smaller scale, mainly because the Germans had largely fled from the territories that belonged to Poland before 1939 before the arrival of the Soviet and the Polish army.

Population transfer resulting from the shifting of the Polish-Soviet and the Polish-German frontier, decided at the Potsdam Conference, was a separate problem. Poles were moving from the Soviet Union to Poland, while Ukrainians, Byelorussians, and Lithuanians were leaving Poland for the Soviet Union. In 1944—46 1.5 million people arrived in Poland from the Soviet Union, while 518,000 Ukrainians, Lithuanians and Byelorussians were repatriated from Poland to the Soviet Union. The post-war transfer of population also included those Germans who stayed in the area between the former Polish-German frontier and the Odra and Lusatian Nysa line; at the end of the war they numbered about 8.5 million; the majority had either been evacuated to the West or had fled from that region, suffering considerable losses in this dramatic period. By the end of July 1945 many Germans had moved on their own initiative to the other bank of the Odra and the Lusatian Nysa, into the Soviet occupation zone, while the planned resettling of Germans to the British and the American zone affected about three million people. They have quickly settled in local society and have come to play a considerable part in the economic development of West Germany.

As a result of all these migrations and the natural increase of the population, Poland had 25 million inhabitants in 1950.

Changes in the Political and Economic System. The Foreign Policy of People's Poland

The 1952 Constitution stated that the Polish People's Republic was a State of people's democracy and that the power belonged to the working people of town and country. That power was to be exercised directly by representatives elected to the Seym and to the people's councils. The social ownership of the basic branches of the national economy and the State monopoly of foreign trade were confirmed. The fundamental tasks of the Seym were to consist in passing laws, supervising public administration, adopting long-term economic plans and approving the State budget. The legislative initiative was vested in the Council of State elected by the Seym, the cabinet and the deputies to the Seym. The cabinet (literally called the Council of Ministers) with its prime minister was to be the highest executive and administrative agency of the State. The Constitution guaranteed to the citizens of People's Poland the right to work, to rest, to the protection of health, to education, and to access to cultural achievements. It also stated that women and men had equal rights, that the State would protect the family as a social institution, that all citizens would enjoy the same rights regardless of nationality, race, and religion, and freedom of conscience. The Church was separated from the State.

Among the socio-economic changes which took place between the merger of the workers' parties and the passing of the 1952 Constitution the most radical was the drive (undertaken despite a shortage of agricultural implements and machines, mainly tractors) to form collective farms. This was intended to unify the agrarian organization of the countries engaged in the building of socialism and rapidly to transform peasant farms concentrating on marketable production on a small scale into socialist ones. The 1952 Constitution included both a provision which promised support to the formation of cooperative farms, and one which ensured protection to individual (private) peasant farms.

The tentative collectivization of agriculture, undertaken in 1949—56, failed to achieve the expected results. At the time when the rapid industrialization of the country was followed by a shortage of consumer goods, among other things, when food rationing was abandoned in January 1953, it was believed that an accelerated socialist reconstruction of agriculture would improve the market situation. This would remove one cause of the dissatisfaction of the workers, which was occasionally making itself felt in social and political life. But the combination of shortage of means of production with sometimes too vigorous promotion of the idea of collective farming, resulted in the failure of those farms to achieve the desired developments. Despite the support of the State authorities, many peasants were alienated from this organizational form of agriculture — to such an extent that 85 per cent of all cooperative farms were dissolved in 1956.

The process was being noted by the authorities of the Polish United Workers' Party with a growing clarity. A new agrarian policy began taking shape at that party's 2nd Congress in March 1954 (preceded by the 9th Plenary Meeting of the Party's Central Committee). The new policy was to consist in the search for diversified methods of socializing agricultural production, with the proviso that such measures should promote the growth of production. It was also decided to increase allocations to agriculture, combined with increased allocations to consumption in general, and a reduction of expenditure on investments.

At the same time the Congress tried to assess critically the influence of the personality cult that was still persisting in the international workers' movement, and to see to it that the provisions of the Constitution concerning socialist democracy were enforced. That implied large-scale participation in the process of government, *inter alia* by work in the Polish United Workers' Party and the allied parties. The point was to ensure the efficient action necessary for the implementation of the very ambitious plan to industrialize the country and thus to lift it out of the backwardness inherited from the past. These ideas could not easily be carried out because many activists of the Polish United Workers' Party still upheld the belief that the class struggle was increasing as socialism was being built, and because of the strong dogmatic tendencies within that party. This led to the preservation of the concept of rightist and nationalist deviation.

The year 1956 saw a new stage in the evolution of political life in Poland. In February of that year the Communist Party of the Soviet Union held its 20th Congress, which revealed the consequences of the personality cult and thus stimulated a more penetrating revaluation of the methods of introducing socialist conditions both in Poland and in other people's democracies. Society at large pressed for the same since it was increasingly disenchanted by the growing problems, falling real wages, insufficient measures intended to raise living standards, bureaucratization of the State agencies, and infringements of the rule of law (for instance, with respect to the former members of the Home Army and to the Church). The measures, undertaken by the PZPR from 1954 on, intended to democratize political life and to raise living standards, proved insufficent, the more so as industrialization and advances in education and culture had resulted in a numerical increase of the working class and a general rise in the political awareness of the nation, which wanted to take a more active part in the process of government and in the programming of social change. This meant that the entire system of the feedback between the national economy, on the one hand, and the social structure and the processes taking place in social consciousness on the other, became extremely intricate. The strike in the Cegielski Works (then called the Stalin Works) in Poznań, which broke out as a result of bureaucratic incompetence and tardiness, was a drastic indicator of the growing contradictions and problems. The strike was not only economic but also political in character and led to mass demonstrations by the inhabitants of Poznań. An attempt to suppress the unrest by force resulted in attacks on public buildings and clashes with security forces, and consequently in casualties. Under those circumstances further steps were taken to restore the socialist rule of law, in which an essential role was played by the 8th Plenary Meeting of the PZPR Central Committee, held in a very tense atmosphere in Warsaw on 19—21 October 1956.

While emphasizing the unchanging observance of the principles of Marxism-Leninism the meeting stressed the necessity of democratizing political life and improving living standards. The concept of the rightist and nationalist deviation was totally abandoned. Władysław Gomułka was elected First Secretary of the Central Committee.

The events in October 1956 created a new political climate in the country and revealed — as had been the case immediately after the end of the war — the spirit of the masses.

Cooperation among the political parties was now reorganized on a partnership basis, the United Peasant Party and the Democratic Party recognizing, however, the leading role of the Polish United Workers' Party.

The Union of Polish Youth, which had experienced a crisis and had been dissolved in January 1957, was replaced by the Union of Socialist Youth and the Union of Peasant Youth, which continued the traditions of the radical youth movement.

A broadly-based socio-political organization, the National Front, formed the Front of National Unity (FJN), in December 1956 with the intention of uniting all strata of the nation. Elections to the Seym were held in January 1957; attendance at the polls was 94.19 per cent, and 94.4 per cent of the votes were cast for the candidates of the Front of National Unity. Poland's position in the international arena was strengthened, and changes in the economic policy at home brought about a rise in living standards. Real wages in 1959 were about one third higher than they had been in 1955. Cultural life became much more dynamic. The political consciousness of the nation increased markedly, and people became determined to eliminate the sectarian tendencies which restricted social activity in general. The programme of a political and economic restructuring of the country won the support of growing numbers of the population. The successive five-year plans (1956—60, 1961—65, 1966—70) meant further advances in the national economy, and the gap between Poland and the highly developed countries was being gradually reduced.

But then it again transpired that it was no easy matter to avoid the contradictions between carrying out production plans and satisfying current needs, i. e., the contradiction between future needs and present needs; this rendered keeping the proper ratio of the accumulation fund to the consumption fund difficult. The development of agriculture proved inadequate in view of the insufficiently flexible agrarian policy. Concentration of efforts on carrying out difficult tasks favoured the growth of centralist tendencies and put a brake on the democratization of public life. The growing population experienced pressing needs in the sphere of housing, yet the authorities tried to resolve the emerging problems by keeping incomes on an unchanged level. The most important decisions were in the hands of a small group of party leaders closely associated with Władysław Gomułka, which caused growing dissatisfaction in party ranks as well. The announcement, shortly before Christmas 1970, of large increases in prices (mainly of meat) resulted in worker demonstrations and strikes, chiefly in Gdańsk and Gdynia, which led to essential corrections in the economic and social policies to take the growing aspirations of the population into account. Dissatisfaction had, by the way, been voiced much earlier, especially during student revolts in March 1968, but the vicious circle was broken only by the 7th Plenary Meeting of the PZPR Central Committee, held in December 1970, which removed from power those who had been responsible for the errors in the economic and social policies and those who, by taking the decision to suppress the unrest by force, caused casualties among the population. Edward Gierek was elected First Secretary; Piotr Jaroszewicz was appointed prime minister, the functions of the chairman of the Council of State being exercised at first by Józef Cyrankiewicz and later by Henryk Jabłoński, professor in Warsaw University and former Secretary General of the Polish Academy of Sciences.

Thus began a new stage of economic development, rapid at the beginning and gradually, in view of excessive centralization and errors in investment policies, slumping in the later period. The living standards rose markedly as a result of increased salaries and wages and a new market policy (for instance, the prices of staple articles of food were frozen for a period of several years). Housing construction was greatly intensified, the agrarian policy advanced the idea of a gradual restructuring of agriculture by supporting those forms of individual farming which brought it closer to socialist economy. The 6th Congress of the PZPR, held in December 1971, stated that increased participation of the working people and their various organizations in the process of government should be one of the main principles of the further development of socialist democracy; it was to serve the common interests of building socialism and to counteract the contradictions which emerge in that process. These directives were confirmed in greater detail at the 7th Party Congress (December 1975), which stressed the importance of better quality of work and a further improvement of living conditions. In 1976, a resolution for amending the Constitution was passed.

The local-governmental administration was reorganized with great costs involved. Poland had been previously divided into 17 voivodships (provinces), with the five largest cities each having, additionally, the status of a voivodship; the voivodships were subdivided into 392 counties and these in turn into 2,365 (rural) communes. Now the number of the voivodships was raised to 49 and the administrative division at the county level was abolished, which added to the status of the rural communes.

The youth movement was united. In 1973 the Federation of Socialist Youth Unions was established.

All these transformations were accompanied by changes in the international situation, marked by the break-up of the colonial system, increased importance of the socialist States, and — after a period of cold war — by the growing tendency to work out the principles of peaceful coexistence among countries with different political systems.

Polish foreign policy had been based on the alliance with the Soviet Union and other socialist States. The Treaty of Friendship, Mutual Aid and Post-war Cooperation of 1945 was renewed in 1965 to cover the next 20 years. The Soviet Union also became Poland's most important partner in all economic matters. Treaties of friendship and cooperation were also concluded with other socialist States.

Quite understandably, relations between Poland and the two German States held a special place in Polish foreign policy. The birth, in 1949, of the German Democratic Republic meant that one part of Germany recognized the consequences of the war started by the Nazi régime, including the acceptance of the Odra and Nysa line as Poland's western frontier. In the so-called Zgorzelec Agreement of 6 July 1950 the German Democratic Republic recognized the existing Polish-German frontier on the Odra and the Lusatian Nysa. At first there were practically no political contacts between Poland and the other German State, i.e. the Federal Republic of Germany, which refused to recognize that frontier. Territorial revisionism and the claim by the Bundesrepublik to be the sole representative of Germany, combined with a policy of negotiation from a position of strength, pursued by Adenauer and his party, could mean only one thing in the eyes of Polish public opinion: German striving for enforcing a change in Poland's western frontier, despite the fact that the frontier had been recognized by the Allies at the Potsdam Conference.

The problems bred by the cold war determined Poland's attitude towards them, and hence also delineated Poland's foreign policy, which consisted in repeated initiatives intended to consolidate international peace and security, to bring about a détente, to limit the arms race, and to promote everything conducive to mutual understanding. Intensified activity in favour of détente in Europe was manifested in Poland's decision to terminate the state of war with Germany (February 1955), the repeated endeavours (1955—57) to establish diplomatic relations with the Federal Republic of Germany, and also suggestions that a non-nuclear zone be created in Central Europe and nuclear armaments frozen. All this culminated in the Polish proposal that a European conference on security and cooperation be convened, submitted on 14 December 1964 at the 19th session of the UN General Assembly.

Cultural and economic contacts between Poland and the Federal Republic of Germany were developing throughout that period, but they intensified only on the strength of an agreement between the two countries, signed in Warsaw on 7 December 1970, concerned with the bases of normalization of relations between Poland and the Federal Republic of Germany: both parties to the agreement confirmed that the existing frontier defined at the Potsdam Conference was the western frontier of Poland. The agreement confirmed the inviolability of existing frontiers in the present and in the future (Art. 1) and declared that the two states had no territorial claims against one another and that they would not advance any such claims in the future. The agreement was an important international event in the post-1945 history of Europe and contributed to détente on that continent. The territorial and political *status quo* in Europe was confirmed in the Final Act of the Conference on Security and Cooperation in Europe, in which 35 European and North American States recognized the inviolability of frontiers to be the fundamental condition of security and peace.

Diplomatic relations between Poland and the Federal Republic of Germany were established in September 1972, following the ratification of the 1970 agreement by the Polish Council of State and the Bundestag. The agreement laid the foundations for normalization of relations between the two countries and made it possible to solve bilateral problems.

The First Secretary of the Central Committee of the PZPR and the Chancellor of the Federal Republic of Germany who met in Helsinki after the signature of the Final Act of the Conference on Security and Cooperation in Europe, decided that a number of agreements would be concluded concerning important issues still pending. These agreements were subsequently signed in Warsaw by the foreign ministers of both countries which confirmed their intention to continue constructively the process of normalization of relations in the spirit of the 1970 agreement. When Edward Gierek visited the Federal Republic of Germany in June 1976 a joint declaration was signed on the development of the relations between the two countries, while a common declaration stating that both sides were ready to continue the process of normalization of relations between them and to conclude new agreements was signed when Helmut Schmidt visited Poland in October 1977. This terminated the first period of the relations between Poland and the Bundesrepublik.

In the history of both countries the 1970s were a period of vigorous development of contacts, in the form of visits of political leaders and parliamentarians and regular consultations between the foreign ministries of the two countries, concerned with bilateral and international issues. There were also meetings of economists, scientists, and journalists, contacts between youth organizations were established, and four Polish and West German cities began to cooperate on a special basis. The problem of bringing separated families together was also successfully solved, following which some 125,000 people left Poland for the Bundesrepublik in 1976—79.

Exchange of tourists increased: in 1979, 303,000 West Germans visited Poland, while over 130,000 Poles saw the Bundesrepublik, which shows that the process was balanced as the West German population is nearly double that of Poland.

While working within the national UNESCO Commissions on school textbooks Polish and West German experts reached agreement on the recommendations to be made concerning the verification of the textbooks for history and geography, used in both countries, so that these textbooks should further the education of the peoples of both countries in the spirit of peace, mutual respect, and trust. In the cultural agreement signed on 11 June 1976, both parties undertook to put these recommendations into effect by correcting the textbooks, but the process has encountered difficulties in the Federal Republic.

The principal obstacle to the normalization of relations between the two countries lies in the fact that the legal consequences of the 1970 agreement (which in the Federal Republic is presented as a *modus vivendi*, or a temporary solution), and hence the recognition of the Odra and Nysa line as an inviolable frontier, are not observed in the legislation and judicial decisions in the Federal Republic of Germany. This is manifested in legal acts which suggest that the German Reich formally continues to exist within the frontiers of 1937. Nor does it contribute to the creation of a proper atmosphere between the two countries if all the persons leaving Poland permanently for the Bundesrepublik are formally assigned there the status of "expelled" persons (*Vertriebene*). The same can be said about the revisionist activity of the organizations of people from the territories now belonging to Poland (*Landsmannschaften*), financed also by the German federal authorities; such organizations reject the 1970 agreement as the basis of normalization of the relations between Poland and the Bundesrepublik.

Industrialization and Social Change. Intensification of National Bonds

The drive for industrialization, launched immediately after the war and particularly intense in the period covered by the Six-Year Plan (1950—56), led to the construction of many new industrial plants (the Lenin Iron and Steel Works in Cracow, the Motorcar Factory in Warsaw, the Lorry Factory in Lublin, and the Chemical Works in Oświęcim), including a number of new industrial town districts, such as Nowa Huta in Cracow, Nowe Tychy and the new districts of Konin in Great Poland. The petrochemical industry was located at Płock, the chemical works in Puławy, Włocławek, Police, and other towns. The coal-mining districts have emerged, such as the Rybnik Coal Basin, the collieries in the Lublin region, still largely under construction, and the brown coal strip mines in the Turoszów region. Sulphur is being extracted in Tarnobrzeg, while copper is mined in

Lubin and Polkowice. The shipbuilding industry has developed remarkably, and a new Port North has been built in Gdańsk. Endeavours were made to industrialize regions with a backward economic structure, but industry in the western and northern territories was expanded, too. The Aluminium Works in Skawina, the Nitrogen Works in Kędzierzyn, the Czechowice Power Plant near Wrocław, and many others were built. In recent years a renewed drive has led to the construction of dozens of new industrial plants, such as the crude oil refinery in Gdańsk, the Katowice Iron and Steel Works, the Piast Coal Mine in Tychy.

In 1973, the level of industrial production in Poland was 20 times higher than it had been in 1938. The structure of industry changed, too: the role of the electrical engineering, chemical, motorcar and shipbuilding industries grew. In terms of per capita production Polish industry reached some four fifths of the level typical of the industrialized countries in Western Europe, and Poland came to rank among the ten most industrialized countries in the world.

In 1950—79, industrial production grew by an averge of 10 per cent annually. Agricultural production increased more slowly, the more so as agriculture provided the principal means that made accumulation, and hence investments, possible. Nevertheless, in the period 1951—75 total agricultural production increased by nearly 90 per cent, the figures being some 75 per cent for plant production and almost 111 per cent for animal production. In 1971—75 alone agricultural production increased by 20 per cent. In the same period, the national income increased by some 60 per cent, the growth of real wages being 41.4 per cent. The average annual rate of growth of agricultural production, taking into account the years marked by poor crops, which recorded a fall of agricultural production in absolute terms, was 3.7 per cent in 1971—75, the analogous figure for 1966—70 being 1.8 per cent. The new agrarian policy, which provided for better supplies of the rural areas with industrial goods, started yielding results. In 1971—75, the socialized sector brought over 750,000 hectares of land under cultivation, so that the socialized economy in 1975 came to account for 29.5 per cent and in 1979 for 31.8 per cent of agricultural land. A large part of that increment came from the land transferred by farmers (especially those too old to work) to the State.

Industrialization and the growth of agriculture were closely linked to changes in the social structure. In that respect People's Poland has witnessed a far reaching revolution. Before the Second World War the rural population accounted for 73 per cent of the population in Poland, whereas in 1979 some 77.5 per cent of the population lived on earnings from non-agricultural sources, the figure being 50 per cent for the rural areas, which means a high degree of urbanization of those areas, accompanied by corresponding changes in cultural patterns. If we take the years 1950, 1960, and 1979, the percentage of the population which lived primarily on agriculture fell from 47.1 to 38.4 and 22.5 per cent, respectively. Correspondingly, the percentage of the urban population was growing rapidly, from 39 in 1950 to 48.3 in 1960 to 58.2 in 1979. While the population of the country increased by 11.7 million people, the corresponding figure for the urban population was 12.5 million, which shows that the towns absorbed not only the whole natural increase of the population, but also some people from the rural areas. The urban population swelled by nearly 3.5 million people between 1971 and 1979 and Poland's urbanization rate equalled those of Austria, Finland, Switzerland and Hungary. We witness the development of conurbations, the most important one being the Gdańsk-Gdynia-Sopot conurbation on the Baltic (with more than 700,000 inhabitants).

In all, the population of Poland rose from 25 million in 1950 to 35.6 million in 1980, which equalled the pre-war level.

Next to the increase of the percentage of the population gainfully employed outside agriculture, the numerical increase of the working class, together with the changes in its structure, must be considered the other significant process. While in 1931 there were 4.2 million workers in all branches of the national economy, of whom less than 30 per cent were employed in industry and the building trade, the figure for 1970 was 6.8 million, of whom 64.5 per cent worked in industry and the building trade. The number of workers employed in modern industries, including the automated ones, has grown to about 40 per cent, many of them educated on the secondary vocational level.

The growth of the intelligentsia is to be noted as the third important change in the social structure, the more so as that group has undergone radical modifications in its nature, primarily because of the higher general standard of education: from being the traditional bearer of the national cultural heritage it has come to be a much more heterogeneous group, comprising the intellectuals, professional people, and the white-collar workers in general; it has also become much less hereditary than before the Second World War. The intelligentsia, decimated by the Nazis, accounted before the war for some 14 per cent of all those gainfully employed outside agriculture; that number rose to some 25 per cent in 1950, and to over 35 per cent in 1973. It now originates mainly from workers (ca. 35 per cent) and peasants (ca. 20 per cent), from the former intelligentsia (ca. 40 per cent), and from among the petit bourgeoisie and the former upper strata of society (ca. 10 per cent). The process, as has been said, is closely associated with the increase in education: while between the two world wars some 85,000 persons acquired higher education, the analogous figure for 1945—65 was 368,900, with an additional 797,800 to be added in the following fourteen years.

The emergence of a modern urban and industrial society was not the only revolutionary change in the realm of social structure. The process has not only put an end to most age-old deformities in the social structure and placed the Polish population in that respect on a par with societies in highly developed countries, but has also penetrated to what might be termed the foundations of the social structure. We mean by this the multidimensional integration of the Polish people which creates a socialist nation. The social changes that occur when socialism is being developed eliminate completely neither the various elements of social differentation, nor contradictions of various kinds. However, this does not invalidate the fundamental significance of the process of integration which forms an intricate network of relationships and mechanisms (not free from conflicts) in the various areas of the life of the nation and the State. Some of these will be mentioned below.

The revolution has brought to an end antagonism between social classes and this has totally changed the nature of the relationships between the State and the people. Further, the westward shifting of the frontiers, both on the east and on the west, has brought about the important macroprocess of cultural adaptation and integration of the various groups of the population on a cross-regional basis, mainly through the spreading of education and culture and through inter-marriages of people from various social and regional groups. In People's Poland, more than five million people have been born in the recovered western and northern territories and this growing number of the genuinely native population must be regarded as the principal strength in the integration, both within the various regions and between each region and the rest of the country.

Industrialization has greatly reduced the differences in the level of development of the various regions and in the pace of the changes taking place in them, and has accordingly led to a territorially more balanced distribution of the working class and of other classes and strata as well, and hence to an increase in the development of social bonds. Further, industrialization, urbanization, increased horizontal social mobility, much quicker flow of information (the radio, TV), the effects of the educational system and advances in cultures, and higher living standards of the rural population — all this has resulted, and continues to result, in reducing the differences between town and country.

The changes in social structure bred new bonds between the various classes and strata and consolidated existing ones. The most important phenomena in this area include the numerical growth within the intelligentsia of the group of technologists, which has yielded closer links between the working class and the intelligentsia. Other facts which are manifestations of integration processes, are associated with what is technically termed breaking down of the characteristics of social status. This means that the three characteristics of social status, namely the nature of work, the level of income, and social prestige, which previously usually accompanied one another, no longer do so; hence a high place in the hierarchy of the prestige of professions and vocations need not correspond to a high incomes level, and vice versa. This brought about an increasingly uniform social structure. On the other hand new social differences emerged due to the redistribution of the national income, profits from additional sources of income, or nepotistic practices resulting in easier access to various goods.

Finally, one of the most important integrating processes appears to be that in social consciousness, the most important feature is that which is common to all and superior to existing differentiations (for example a division into believers and non-believers). The growing number of those elements of social consciousness that are common to all, which is an effect of the historical experience of the nation, is decisive and indispensable for conscious collective actions. These elements of social consciousness, which are common to most people after the Second World War, include the acceptance of the present frontiers of the State, and the vision of the State in which the masses with the working class and its political party play the dominant political and social role; also acceptance of the programme of social and economic reconstruction, belief in the importance of education and science, and active participation in cultural life.

Education, Science, Culture and Artistic Life

Broadly speaking, cultural life has played a major role in defining the processes of integration described above. In most general terms, life has become in a sense urbanized, which can best be seen in the rural areas. The process has had two features: the adaptation of the people from the rural areas who have moved to towns to the patterns of urban life, and the penetration by those patterns into rural life. Traditional folk culture has begun to vanish and changed into "folklore" in the sense of something "ornamental", deliberately revitalized in order to exploit local colour. The most visible changes are observable in rural housing construction which frequently imitates second rate urban models, while folk patterns have become popular with well-to-do town dwellers. The same applies to furniture. Here, modernization in the rural area reached stoves and ovens first, spreading gradually to furniture and various household appliance (no more benches and chests, changes in interior decoration). There has been a general trend to increase floor space, also in towns, where — after the first period of reconstruction — housing conditions have been improving, though at too slow a pace.

Efforts have been made to improve the functioning of public utilities in towns and to embellish urban centres, also to adapt them to the growing number of motorcars. The car known as the Polski Fiat 126 p has begun to contribute to the development of tourism, with all the accompanying changes in the way of life. Farms have ceased to be self-supporting units in matters of food production. Even more striking changes have taken place in the sphere of dress; in this respect the differences between town and country have vanished for all practical purposes, except that in some regions folk costumes are still being worn on festive occasions; this has consequently led to the adoption by the inhabitants of the rural areas of fashion trends prevailing in the western world. Obliteration of the differences between town and country in the aspects discussed above took place between 1950 and 1960, especially in household equipment and the ways young people dress. Sports and tourism have become popular in the rural areas.

In the post-war period facilities for intellectual pursuits became increasingly available, for example, the number of libraries and museums has grown.

The Manifesto of the Polish Committee of National Liberation announced that the school system would be expanded and the intelligentsia given special protection, which was to be accompanied by the democratization of culture. This programme envisaged a *sui generis* revolution in the sphere of national culture. The enormous work in this field began with the removal of secondary illiteracy (caused by the conditions prevailing under the Nazi occupation). As Bolesław Bierut put it when speaking at the opening of the radio broadcasting station in Wrocław on 16 November 1947, the popularization and socialization of cultural production in all its fields and manifestations was the task set the present generation of the makers of culture and the entire nation by the new period of our history, that of people's democracy.

When speaking about the development of cultural life in the broad sense of the word, it is important to remember the role played in the early period of People's Poland by the town of Lublin where many daily papers and periodicals were published. Lublin at that time was also the centre of a vigorous theatrical life (with such outstanding actors as Jan Kreczmar, Jacek Woszczerowicz, Władysław Krasnowiecki, Jan Świderski, and Aleksander Zelwerowicz), a strong literary milieu (with Mieczysław Jastrun, Julian Przyboś, Jerzy Putrament and Adam Ważyk), and an important centre of academic activity (with the first universities to be opened after the Nazi occupation, namely the newly founded Maria Curie-Skłodowska University and the Roman Catholic University).

Next the role of the Polish cultural centre was taken over by Łódź, with the periodicals *Kuźnica* and *Myśl Współczesna* and a strong academic centre with such eminent scholars as Tadeusz Kotarbiński, Stanisław Ossowski, Maria Ossowska, Józef Chałasiński, and Natalia Gąsiorowska. Theatrical life was very active here, with stage directors Leon Schiller and Juliusz Osterwa, and also those who had moved there from Lublin.

All this did not last long, because following the reconstruction of Warsaw, enthusiastically supported by all (as was later, in 1970, the idea of rebuilding the Royal Castle in Warsaw), the centre of cultural and academic life moved to the capital, which soon regained its leading position.

Wrocław also became a strong cultural and academic centre, which in some fields (mathematics with Hugo Steinhaus and Edward Marczewski and haematology with Ludwik Hirszfeld) soon won international renown. Literary life flourished too. That the World Congress 'Intellectuals for Peace' was held in Wrocław in 1948 testifies to Wrocław's rank in intellectual life. Cracow was very active, too, with a number of university schools and was an important publishing centre. The local theatres (at that time with the stage director Arnold Szyfman and actors Ludwik Solski and Karol Adwentowicz) were at a traditionally high level.

Szczecin was slower to emerge as an intellectual centre: the process required the development of a kind of regional identity by the people who settled there from other parts of the country. Zielona Góra and such towns as Toruń, Opole, Olsztyn, Białystok, Rzeszów, Bydgoszcz, Koszalin and Słupsk also appeared on the cultural map of Poland, with their own intellectual centres. Several prominent writers, scholars and artists began their career in Poznań which had a considerable share in the animation of post-war cultural life.

Cultural cooperation developed at first primarily with the Soviet Union and other socialist countries. Contacts with other countries were also being gradually established.

Education was the basis on which culture could develop and spread. Visions of the post-war system of education were mapped out as early as the Nazi occupation, e. g., by the Clandestine Organization of Teachers. It was to them that the Congress on Education, held in Łódź in June 1945, referred when the model of education in Poland was discussed. But discussions and modifications were numerous. The post-war period witnessed a growth in the number of schools and pupils: in 1945/46 there were 18,397 schools with three million pupils, and in 1949/50, 22,738 schools with 3.4 million pupils. The number of schools of higher education (both vocational and those of the university standing) rose from 46 (with 56,000 students) in 1945/46 to 67 (with 115,000 students) in 1949/50.

The circulation of newspapers increased from 1,118,000 copies daily in 1945 to 4,199,000 copies in 1949. The centralization of cultural life, observable after 1948, led to a reduction of the number of periodicals, but with an increase in the total number of copies. The press came to be avidly read in the rural areas, and many periodicals for the national minorities appeared. The production of books rose from 1,083 titles with a total impression of 10 million copies in 1945 to 4,611 titles with a total impression of 118 million copies in 1950.

The radio broadcasting system, completely destroyed by the Nazis, developed rapidly: in 1948 the number of receivers almost equalled the pre-war level; electrification of the rural areas, which gradually covered the whole country, led to an increase in the number of radio receivers there. This last applies to TV sets as well, when TV broadcasts were started in the 1950s.

The state enterprise Film Polski, established in 1945, helped the cinematic art develop rapidly. Audiences were growing, and Polish films began to win recognition abroad. The first Polish post-war film, *Forbidden Songs* concerned with the Nazi occupation and first shown in Warsaw on 8 January 1947, aroused lively discussion. People in the rural areas also started clamouring for cinemas and films.

The centralist tendencies in cultural life were overcome to a considerable extent in 1954—56, which stimulated cultural activity again. The number of pupils in secondary schools increased from over 0.5 million in 1950/51 to 2.4 million in 1979/80; in the same period the number of students in schools of university status rose from 125,000 to nearly 500,000 in the 1970s. This illustrates the scale of the spreading of post-elementary education, and hence the better intellectual "equipment" of the population. In 1979/80 Poland had 10 universities, 18 colleges (institutes) of technology, 10 medical academies, nine agricultural academies, and 46 schools of other types (concerned with teacher training, physical education and sports, art, and theology).

The Polish Academy of Sciences, which now has branches in Cracow, Poznań, Wrocław, Katowice, and Łódź, and also research centres in France and Italy, was founded at the First Congress of Polish Science, held in Warsaw in 1951. Over 100 research institutes attached to the various ministries have been set up. The number of research workers increased signally; while the average rise in employment in the socialized economy was 7.6 per cent between 1970 and 1972, the analogous figure for the number of researchers and the academic staff was 55.7 per cent.

In many fields Polish science has won international renown; Polish scientists have striven to solve problems related to the rapid development of the country. Mathematics is among those disciplines which have won the greatest renown on an international scale; research in new branches has been added to that in the branches for which this country had been famous already before the Second World War (mathematical logic, set theory, topology). Notable achievements have been recorded in theoretical and nuclear physics and in optics. People's Poland has seen considerable advances in the technical sciences, geography, the biological sciences, sociology. In medicine, which has remarkable achievements to its credit, the pride of place goes to immunology, haematology, human genetics, orthopaedics, ophthalmic surgery, and pharmacology. The restructuring of agriculture has stimulated advances in the agricultural sciences.

In the social sciences, the methodological and theoretical inspirations of Marxism combined with the traditionally high standard of rigour in research have resulted in unprecedented attainments. Great progress has been noted in the methodology of sciences, drawing on the work of such past masters in that field as Tadeusz Kotarbiński and Kazimierz Ajdukiewicz. Sociologists have been given a laboratory on an immense scale in the form of study of the changes taking place in this country. Economics can boast of such scientists of international renown as Oskar Lange and Michał Kalecki. Important advances have been made in jurisprudence, also inspired by the problems emerging from a new political and economic system, special mention being due to international law, civil law, constitutional and legal theory, and legal history. Classical philology and Oriental studies have also reached international standards. Historical studies, which have had a long tradition in this country, marked a new stage in their development and gave rise to "the Polish school in historiography"; they are probably the most expanded branch of the humanities in Poland. Art history received a considerable stimulus in connection with the need to restore works of art destroyed or damaged during the hostilities and the Nazi occupation. Polish archaeology and the history of material civilization are widely known abroad. Literary studies, art history, and aesthetics also developed at a fair pace. There are regular and lively contacts between Polish and foreign scholars, in both socialist and capitalist countries.

Literary works have had a traditionally strong impact upon the formation of human attitudes. Next to 19th century classics the most widely read authors include Maria Dąbrowska, Jarosław Iwaszkiewicz, Jan Parandowski, Władysław Broniewski, Stanisław Lem, Konstanty Ildefons Gałczyński, and Tadeusz Różewicz. These are accompanied by such equally prestigious authors as Jerzy Andrzejewski, Kazimierz Brandys, Tadeusz Breza, Stanisław Dygat, Bogdan Czeszko, Stanisław Grochowiak, Andrzej Kuśniewicz, Sławomir Mrożek, Teodor Parnicki, Julian Tuwim, and Wojciech Żukrowski. Some of the most renowned Polish authors have been living and writing abroad; they include the late Witold Gombrowicz and Kazimierz Wierzyński, and Czesław Miłosz, who was awarded the Nobel Prize in 1980. Polish literature has been greatly influenced by the experiences acquired during the Second World War and the Nazi occupation of the country, and also by the impact of the changes that have taken place here after 1945. This is why the novel, with the opportunities for description it offers, has been the most important literary genre.

In Polish films, too, the same experiences, the history of the nation, and recent transformations have been decisive for the subject matter of the works produced by Andrzej Wajda, Andrzej Munk, Jerzy Kawalerowicz, Krzysztof Zanussi, and many others.

Many Polish architects have won international fame by winning first prizes in many competitions. The most important personalities in sculpture include Xawery Dunikowski, Stanisław Horno-Popławski, Marian Wnuk, Antoni Kenar, Alina Szapocznikow, and Władysław Hasior; in painting, the same may be said about Jan Cybis, Eugeniusz Eibisch, and Stefan Gierowski. The graphic arts and poster design have also contributed important achievements.

A special mention is due to the Polish theatre which has made itself known throughout the world. Perhaps the pride of place in that respect goes to Wrocław with its Laboratory Theatre run by Jerzy Grotowski and the Pantomime Theatre under Henryk Tomaszewski. Warsaw with its 35 professional theatres is the largest centre in the country's theatrical life, followed by Cracow, which, however, is given by critics the first place in originality in the approaches to stage direction. The most important stage directors include Kazimierz Dejmek, Adam Hanuszkiewicz, Andrzej Wajda, Józef Szajna, and the late Konrad Swinarski.

Music has been developing vigorously; already by 1948 there were six philharmonic halls, eight symphony orchestra houses, and four opera houses; by 1956 the numbers of the symphony orchestra houses had risen to 27, and that of the opera houses to nine, to which eight musical and operetta theatres were added. In the first post-war decade many important compositions were largely inspired by Polish folk culture (those by Stanisław Wiechowicz, Jan Maklakiewicz, Witold Lutosławski, Kazimierz Serocki, and others). A different type of music was represented by Bolesław Szabelski, Zbigniew Turski, Grażyna Bacewicz, Tadeusz Baird, and Bolesław Woytowicz. Contacts with the trends prevailing abroad became closer after 1956, and the Autumn Festivals of Modern Music, held annually in Warsaw, have become the most comprehensive presentations of modern music in the world, which also ushered in Krzysztof Penderecki, Henryk Górecki, Zygmunt Krauze, and others. The Chopin competition and the Wieniawski competition are being held regularly in Warsaw and Poznań, respectively. Works by Krzysztof Penderecki, Witold Lutosławski and Tadeusz Baird rank among major achievements in world music. Mention must also be made of outstanding conductors, such as Grzegorz Fitelberg, Walerian Bierdiajew, Henryk Czyż, Kazimierz Kord, Jan Krenz, Andrzej Markowski, Witold Rowicki, Robert Satanowski, Stanisław Skrowaczewski, Bohdan Wodiczko, and Stanisław Wisłocki, and of singers including Andrzej Hiolski, Teresa Kubiak, Bernard Ładysz, Wiesław Ochman, Stefania Woytowicz and Teresa Żylis-Gara, pianists such as Halina Czerny-Stefańska, Barbara Hesse-Bukowska, Adam Harsiewicz, Lidia Grychtołówna, Władysław Kędra and Krystian Zimerman, and violinists including Wanda Wiłkomirska, Konstanty Andrzej Kulka, and Kaja Danczowska.

Cultural life in Poland is varied and marked by a creative search for novel elements. Active participation in culture is facilitated by the various institutions whose special task is to offer opportunities to the public, especially the young people, for direct contacts with artistic production. In 1979, there were 20,000 such centres, including 2,176 community centres and 18,000 clubs of various kinds, with more than 40,000 amateur groups (with a total membership of over 700,000 people).

Cultural and educational activity is promoted by the Popular

Knowledge Society, which organizes various lectures and cour-
ses, attended in 1974 by some six million people.

Following the great acceleration in the sphere of cultural development observable in the post-war years and the above-mentioned blossoming of cultural initiatives after 1956, there came
recurrently more difficult periods for culture. Processes of industrialization rather over-occupied the attention of those who
handed out the funds for culture for them to devote to the latter
the attention that the assumptions of the democratization of the
cultural process required. Due to this, particularly in the 1970s
the pulse of cultural life weakened, editions of books decreased
in number, the amount of textbooks printed and records
produced was insufficient, the circulation of newspapers, weeklies
and other magazines dwindled. A contradiction outlined itself
between the assumptions of the continuing democratization of
culture and the real conditions of its development, which limited the possibilities of participation in culture for the ordinary
citizen. This was not visible in an obvious way on the outside.
The international prestige of Polish science and culture held
fast.

In 1978, the Polish nation celebrated the 60th anniversary of its
independence regained after 120 years of national servitude.
This anniversary was treated as an opportunity for paying attention to a historical moment that must be interpreted in its historical context. History is a continuous process; it is a continuation of the past combined with ever new developmental stages. The rise in Polish prestige has been a continuous process.
The choice, in 1978, of the Polish cardinal Karol Wojtyła as
Pope — John Paul II — is also evidence of this.

Activation of the Working Class in 1980.
The Beginning of a New Stage in the Development
of the Polish People's Republic

The vigorous economic and cultural development that followed
the changes in the leadership of the Polish United Workers'
Party and in the government in December 1970 was considerably slowed in the mid-1970s. Managerial methods were not
adjusted to the ambitious plans of rapidly modernizing the national economy and raising living standards. Nor was there any
development of the democratic system to increase the real participation of the working people in the government of the coun-

try, as had been announced in the resolution adopted by the Sixth Congress of the Polish United Workers' Party. This led to intensifying conflicts between the growing political consciousness of the Polish people, the aspirations of the growing working class, the development of industry, the general needs of the population and the requirements of an intensive development of national culture, on the one hand, and on the other the possibilities of having those needs and aspirations satisfied, both in their economic and socio-political aspect. A qualitatively new process was the consolidation of the working class, now widely different from the working class of the 1950s, i.e. at the time of the vast industrialization processes, still not unified and deeply rooted in the peasant tradition.

Tendencies to run the national economy in a bureaucratic manner, preventing the proper implementation of the economic plans and the internal mechanisms, such as the requirements of the market, that helped restore economic equilibrium, prevailed in the Polish United Workers' Party and the government. This was why the slow-down, in the late 1970s, of economic activity, also palpable in other socialist countries and party due to the trends in the world economy, was particularly marked in Poland. The efficiency of the national economy decreased, which was combined with a decline in the stimulating role of foreign credits, which — as it turned out — should have been paid back before the investments for which they had been contracted started yielding the expected benefits. There was a growing number of arbitrary decisions concerned with investments, which disregarded the actual possibilities and economic calculations. This intensified inflationary tendencies and worsened the conditions prevailing in the market. The increase in wages was levelled down and often preceded by a growth in prices, while the shortages in market supply had an additionally adverse effect on the population's living conditions and labour productivity. Such negative phenomena also appeared in agriculture and the situation of the rural population. Growing difficulties were followed by increasing centralization of economic and political life and restrictions imposed upon the democratic system. The role of the trade unions was drastically reduced. At the same time the mass media continued the propaganda of success, which was less and less confirmed by facts. This situation had an adverse effect upon cultural life. The number of books published fell considerably. Critical opinions voiced in the central authorities of the Polish United Workers' Party were being suppressed, and the growing dissatisfaction in society at large was disregarded.

All this led to a crisis. It found its most acute and widely spread form in the wave of spontaneous strikes that swept the country in August 1980, and were most intensified in the coastal region (Gdańsk, Szczecin, Elbląg). These strikes expressed the workers' dissatisfaction with the degeneration and distortions in political, social and economic life. The working class came forward with demands for restoring to it the right to decide on the nation's most important problems and to influence the methods of functioning of the supreme state organs.

These demands, which were negotiated with representatives of the supreme state authorities, became the foundation of the agreements signed by the government commissions and the inter-factory strike committees in Gdańsk, Szczecin and Jastrzębie. Of these the most important was the one concerning the establishment of independent trade unions which were to guarantee the implementation of the agreements.

Following sharp criticism, personal changes in the Polish United Workers' Party and the government took place. Those responsible for the crisis were dismissed. The 4th plenary meeting of the Central Committee removed Edward Gierek from the post of the First Secretary of the Polish United Workers' Party (Piotr Jaroszewicz was dismissed from the office of Prime Minister before the August events).

The agreements from Gdańsk, Szczecin and Jastrzębie constitute in themselves an ambitious programme of reform and, accompanied by the foundation of the free and independent trade unions, generated social processes of an unusual power, scale and range. The Seym of the Polish People's Republic demanded the restoration of its constitutional rights and began to wield genuine control of the government's work. The Supreme Chamber of Control became subordinated to the Seym. Far-reaching changes took place in the methods of work of the supreme party and government authorities. Work started on economic reform and draft laws on censorship, trade unions, self-governing bodies and enterprises. Genuine consulation on new laws with the trade unions, creative associations and society as a whole was initiated. A new stage in the country's development began.

Jerzy Topolski

List of Illustrations

178

38. Aleksander Orłowski, *Slaughter at Praga (Warsaw)*
    National Museum in Cracow, Czartoryski Collections. Phot. Jerzy Myszkowski
39. Marcello Bacciarelli, *Napoleon Granting the Constitution to the Duchy of Warsaw*
    Wilanów Museum in Warsaw. Phot. Jerzy Myszkowski
40. Henryk Pillati, *Death of Berek Yoselevich at Kock*
    National Museum in Warsaw. Phot. Jerzy Myszkowski
41. Piotr Michałowski, *The Battle of Somosierra*
    National Museum in Cracow. Phot. Jerzy Myszkowski
42. January Suchodolski, *The Death of Cyprian Godebski at Raszyn*
    National Museum in Warsaw. Phot. Jerzy Myszkowski
43. Jan Nepomucen Bizański, *The Raising of the Kosciuszko Mound in Cracow*
    National Museum in Cracow. Phot. Jerzy Myszkowski
44. Anonymous, after Horace Vernet, *Death of Prince Joseph Poniatowski*
    National Museum in Cracow. Phot. Jerzy Myszkowski
45. Wincenty Kasprzycki, *Fine Art Exhibition in Warsaw in 1828*
    National Museum in Warsaw. Phot. Jerzy Myszkowski
46. Marcin Zaleski, *The Capture of the Arsenal*
    Historical Museum of the City of Warsaw. Phot. Jerzy Myszkowski
47. Wojciech Kossak, *The Battle of Olszynka Grochowska*
    Polish Army Museum in Warsaw. Phot. Mirosław Ciunowicz
48. Teofil Kwiatkowski, *A Ball in the Hôtel Lambert in Paris*
    National Museum in Poznań. Phot. Jerzy Myszkowski
49. Michał Stachowicz, *Harvest-home Festival*
    National Museum in Warsaw. Phot. Jerzy Myszkowski
50. Anonymous, *The Galician Slaughter of 1846*
    Polish Army Museum in Warsaw. Phot. Mirosław Ciunowicz
51. Artur Grottger, *Farewell to an Insurgent*
    National Museum in Cracow. Phot. Jerzy Myszkowski
52. Artur Grottger, *Welcome to an Insurgent*
    National Museum in Cracow. Phot. Jerzy Myszkowski
53. Jan Matejko, *Poland Enfettered*
    National Museum in Cracow, Czartoryski Collections. Phot. Jerzy Myszkowski
54. Jacek Malczewski, *On the Etape*
    National Museum in Poznań. Phot. Jerzy Myszkowski
55. Jacek Malczewski, *Melancholy*
    National Museum in Poznań. Phot. Jerzy Myszkowski
56. Aleksander Gierymski, *Sand-diggers*
    National Museum in Warsaw. Phot. Jerzy Myszkowski
57. Kazimierz Alchimowicz, *Hire of Farm Hands*
    National Museum in Warsaw. Phot. Jerzy Myszkowski
58. Stanisław Lentz, *Strike*
    National Museum in Warsaw. Phot. Jerzy Myszkowski

59. Michał Bylina, *The Red Regiment of Warsaw*
    Polish Army Museum in Warsaw. Phot. Mirosław Ciunowicz
60. Stanisław Bargiełowski, *The Disarming of Germans in Warsaw*
    Polish Army Museum in Warsaw. Phot. Mirosław Ciunowicz
61. Michał Bylina, *September 1939*
    Polish Army Museum in Warsaw. Phot. Mirosław Ciunowicz
62. Andrzej Wróblewski, *Firing Squad*
    National Museum in Warsaw. Phot. Jerzy Myszkowski
63. Jerzy Krawczyk, *A Worthless Cargo*
    Museum of Art in Łódź. Phot. Jerzy Myszkowski
64. Andrzej Wróblewski, *Partisans*
    National Museum in Warsaw. Phot. Jerzy Myszkowski
65. Stanisław Poznański, *Soldiers of the Kosciuszko Division Taking the Oath*
    Polish Army Museum in Warsaw. Phot. Mirosław Ciunowicz
66. Michał Bylina, *The Battle of Lenino*
    Polish Army Museum in Warsaw. Phot. Mirosław Ciunowicz
67. Stefan Garwatowski, *Hill 593*
    Polish Army Museum in Warsaw. Phot. Mirosław Ciunowicz
68. Marcin Szczerba, *A Dying City*
    Polish Army Museum in Warsaw. Phot. Mirosław Ciunowicz
69. Aleksander Kobzdej, *Pass Me a Brick*
    National Museum in Warsaw. Phot. Jerzy Myszkowski
70. Helena Krajewska, *A Youth Brigade Breaking a Record on the Building Site*
    National Museum in Warsaw. Phot. Jerzy Myszkowski
71. Juliusz Krajewski, *Land for the Peasants*
    Lenin Museum in Cracow. Phot. Jerzy Myszkowski
72. Andrzej Feliks Szumigraj, *Worker's Head*
    Museum of History of Revolutionary Movements in Warsaw. Phot. Jerzy Myszkowski

Zakłady Graficzne RSW ,,Prasa-Książka-Ruch"
Wrocław, ul. Piotra Skargi 3/5